T3-BPE-232

PERGAMON INTERNATIONAL LIBRARY
of Science, Technology, Engineering and Social Studies
*The 1000-volume original paperback library in aid of education,
industrial training and the enjoyment of leisure*

Publisher: Robert Maxwell, M.C.

The Evaluation of Risk
in Business Investment

The Evaluation of Risk in Business Investment

by

J. C. HULL, M.A., Ph.D.

Cranfield School of Management

PERGAMON PRESS

OXFORD · NEW YORK · TORONTO · SYDNEY · PARIS · FRANKFURT

U.K.	Pergamon Press Ltd., Headington Hill Hall, Oxford OX3 0BW, England
U.S.A.	Pergamon Press Inc., Maxwell House, Fairview Park, Elmsford, New York 10523, U.S.A.
CANADA	Pergamon of Canada, Suite 104, 150 Consumers Road, Willowdale, Ontario M2J 1P9, Canada
AUSTRALIA	Pergamon Press (Aust.) Pty. Ltd., P.O. Box 544, Potts Point, N.S.W. 2011, Australia
FRANCE	Pergamon Press SARL, 24 rue des Ecoles, 75240 Paris, Cedex 05, France
FEDERAL REPUBLIC OF GERMANY	Pergamon Press GmbH, 6242 Kronberg/Taunus, Hammerweg 6, Federal Republic of Germany

First edition 1980

British Library Cataloguing in Publication Data

Hull, J C
The evaluation of risk in business investment —
(Pergamon international library).
1. Capital investments
2. Risk
I. Title
658.1'527   HG4028.C4   80–40136

ISBN 0–08–024075–5
ISBN 0–08–024074–7 Pbk

ISBN 0 08 024075 5   Hardcover
ISBN 0 08 024074 7   Flexicover

*Printed and bound in Great Britain by
William Clowes (Beccles) Limited, Beccles and London*

Contents

List of Tables

List of Figures

Preface

The importance of taking risk into account in capital investment appraisal is now widely recognized by both practising managers and the academic community. Many different approaches to the problem have been suggested, varying greatly in their level of sophistication. This book provides finance specialists in industry and students of management with a comprehensive set of practical procedures, involving sensitivity analyses and simulations, for evaluating investment risk.

The emphasis is on the quantification of an investment's *total* risk. This is a little out of line with modern financial theory which advocates that the capital asset pricing model be used to value an investment opportunity's uncertain cash flows, from the point of view of a well-diversified shareholder. The justification for the approach adopted here is, first, that many company managers still place a high premium on evaluating the total risk in an investment opportunity and, second, that a good measure of total risk is often a necessary prerequisite to an examination of the extent to which the risk can be "diversified away" by the company or its shareholders.

Chapter 1 discusses traditional DCF methods. In Chapter 2, analytic and simulation approaches to risk evaluation are described. Chapter 3 considers how managers make predictions about the variables affecting the performance of an investment, and critically examines the different procedures for assessing subjective probability distributions. Chapter 4 focuses on the problems arising from dependences between variables and provides a number of practical guide-lines as to how they can be overcome. Chapter 5 presents some fairly new ideas on how rough measures of the total riskiness of an investment can be produced from the output of a sensitivity analysis. Chapter 6 considers the decision tree approach to coping with sequential investment decisions. Chapter 7 reviews some of the theoretical developments in our understanding of the nature of investment risk over the last 15 years, discussing utility theory, portfolio theory and the capital asset pricing model. Chapter 8 provides a case study which draws together many of the arguments and methodologies presented in earlier chapters. Finally, Chapter 9 considers the behavioural problems of introducing risk evaluation into an organisation and how they can be overcome.

The emphasis throughout the book is on "how to do it" and practising financial managers should find the computer programs described in Appendices A and B particularly useful. The programs can be used as they stand or modified to suit the user's requirements. With the exception of Appendix C (which discusses a particular approach to dealing with dependent random variables), mathematical and statistical formulae and arguments should not cause the average reader undue difficulty.

Much of this book is based on my PhD thesis which was finished at Cranfield in 1976. I would like to record my appreciation of the help and encouragement which I received at all times from my thesis supervisor, Ron Adelson of Lancaster University. Brian Wheeler at Cranfield provided useful advice on the development of the computer subroutines. The book has also benefited from numerous discussions I have had with industrialists, academic colleagues (particularly Professor D. R. Myddelton) and MBA students over a number of years. The responsibility for the finished product is of course my own.

June 1980   JOHN HULL

Chapter 1

BASIC PRINCIPLES OF INVESTMENT APPRAISAL

1.1. Introduction

It is sometimes said that financial management is about "getting money and spending it". This description, although a little terse, is essentially accurate. Part of the subject is concerned with investigating the different long- and short-term sources of funds available to a company so that an appropriate financing mix can be chosen; part is concerned with using the funds in the best way possible within the company. Funds can be used for either short- or long-term purposes. The short-term use of funds to build up stocks, provide customers with more credit, etc., is the subject of working capital management. The long-term allocation of funds to major capital investment projects is known as capital budgeting and is the subject of this book.

At the outset it is worth noting that we shall use the term capital investment in a rather different way from the accountant. An accountant distinguishes between revenue and capital expenditures. The former are charged against profits as soon as they are incurred; the latter are capitalised, shown on the balance sheet as fixed assets and often depreciated over a period of time. Typically, investments in land, plant and machinery are capitalised while R and D expenditures (except those on fixed assets) and, at the time of writing, lease commitments, are not. We shall use the term capital investment to cover rather more than just that which is capitalised by the accountant. Any long-term major allocation of funds will be considered to be a capital investment. Thus a 5-year training programme or a major advertising campaign or an investment in R and D, although they might not be capitalised on the balance sheet, all come within the ambit of what is to be discussed in the pages which follow.

Capital investment decisions are among the most important which a company makes. Very often they involve a relatively large commitment of a company's resources and are instrumental in shaping its whole future. To a large extent the expenditures which capital budgeting decisions involve are irreversible. Once a company has committed itself to building a new plant or promoting a new product it cannot easily turn back. Inadequate though the return may be, it may still be better to continue with a project than accept low abandonment values. In contrast, working capital management decisions are usually reversible. For example, if management invests too much in stocks then a cut-back in production will usually correct the situation within a matter of months.

The problems of capital investment have become more acute in recent years. The increasing rate of technological change has meant that new plant and machinery is now liable to become obsolescent in a relatively short period of time. Both consumer and industrial markets have become more volatile. The actions of competitors have become less predictable. In short, the risk in nearly all major capital investments is now far greater than ever before. This book is concerned with the systematic procedures which can be used to evaluate (and sometimes reduce) risk.

The present chapter is concerned with setting the scene. First the basic approaches to evaluating capital investment projects are presented. The discussion then focuses on risk, and the basic idea that the expected return which the provider of funds to a business requires is related to the riskiness of the return.

1.2. Measuring Costs and Benefits

Capital investment decisions nearly always involve immediate outlays in order to achieve future benefits. This raises two important conceptual problems: how should the outlays and benefits be measured and how should they be compared. This section will deal with the first of these problems, while the next section will tackle the second.

Investment outlays should clearly be measured in terms of their cash amount. As far as the benefits from the investment are concerned, the main issue is whether they should be measured in terms of profits or cash flows. It is now fairly widely accepted that the use of cash flows is correct. It is always the cash flowing into or out of a business as a result of an investment, together with the timing of these cash flows, that is relevant when a decision on the investment is being made. Profits are to an extent an accounting abstraction; they depend on the company's depreciation policy, stock valuation method, and so on. When taking a capital budgeting decision a company is interested in whether it will be able to repay capital and provide investors with an adequate rate of interest. Both capital and interests can only be paid directly out of cash flows — not profits.

In the case of large investments the effect on profits should not be ignored. This is because for the most part it is profits which are communicated to shareholders, and profits which are used in calculating the widely used earnings per share figures. However, it should always be borne in mind that there can be significant time differences between profits being reported in a company's accounts and the corresponding cash flows actually occurring.

It is worth stressing at this point that a company should be interested in the *incremental* cash flows arising from a project. That is, it should be interested in:

(a) Cash flows which will occur if the project is undertaken but which will not occur otherwise; and

(b) Cash flows which will occur if the project is not undertaken but which will not occur if it is undertaken.

The net cash flow figure which is calculated for a year should indicate the difference between the position the company will be in if it goes ahead with the investment, and the position it will be in if it does not. Cash flows which will occur regardless of the investment decision are clearly irrelevant. It should be remembered that we are only interested in future cash flows. Those which have already been incurred are "sunk" and should be ignored. Thus, if a company spent £100,000 on a new machine last year and is wondering whether to replace it this year with a newer model, the £100,000 is irrelevant. The relevant factors are likely to be the disposal value of the existing machine, the cost of the newer model, the saving in operating costs, etc. These all give rise to changes in the company's *future* cash flows.

The cash flows which are calculated should *not* reflect the cost of financing a project. The interest on any debt which is raised and the dividends to be paid on any new equity capital are not project cash flows for the purposes of investment appraisal. A company's cost of capital is generally taken account of by the way in which the performance measure is calculated and used. Combining financing cash flows with the project's other cash flows would result in double counting.

A further general principle is that cash flows should always be measured on an after-tax basis, i.e. a company's incremental tax cash flows should always be included in any analysis. It is inaccurate to use a method of project evaluation based on pre-tax cash flows. Tax affects different projects in different ways. For example, in the UK at the time of writing most plant and machinery can, for tax purposes, be entirely written off against profits in the first year of operations; while investments in factories give rise to only 50% first year tax allowances (the other 50% being allowed over a period of 13 years) and investments in office blocks give rise to no tax allowances at all.

One last point to be raised in the context of measuring costs and benefits concerns inflation. A company should recognise that cash flows can be estimated in either present day £s (i.e. ignoring inflationary increases) or in the £ figures which are considered likely to occur after a full allowance has been made for inflation. Naturally the parameters of the evaluation method which is chosen must depend on the choice which is made here. This point will be considered further later in this chapter.

1.3.   Performance Measures

Several different measures of investment performance are currently used by industry. The most important are the payback period, the accounting rate of return, the net present value and the internal rate of return. Each of these will be discussed in turn in this section. The following notation will be used:

n = the life of the project in years

C_i = the net cash flow in year i ($i = 0, 1, 2 \ldots n$).

(By convention, C_0 is the net cash flow incurred at the start of the project, C_1 is the net cash flow during the first year, C_2 is the net cash flow during the second year, etc.)

The payback period method, partly because of its simplicity, is very popular with businessmen. The payback period is calculated as the number of years necessary for the investment to generate sufficient positive cash flows to cover the early negative cash outlays. An investment which involved an initial cash outlay of £160,000 and generated positive cash flows of £80,000 per year for 4 years would have a payback period of 2 years. Companies often require projects to have a payback period of less than 2 to 3 years.

The disadvantages of payback can be illustrated with reference to the 4 projects in Table 1. First, the method ignores cash flows after the end of the payback period and would not discriminate between projects A and B even though B is clearly superior by virtue of its longer life. Second, the method ignores the timing of cash flows during the payback period and would not discriminate between projects B and C even though B is clearly preferable. Third, the method only considers the magnitudes of cash flows relative to each other, and would not distinguish between B and D even though the financial consequences of B are ten times as great of those of D.

TABLE 1. EXAMPLES OF DIFFERENT PROJECTS

Year	Cash flow from project			
	A	B	C	D
0	−160	−160	−160	−16
1	+ 80	+ 80	+ 20	+ 8
2	+ 80	+ 80	+140	+ 8
3	..	+ 80	+ 80	+ 8
4	..	+ 80	+ 80	+ 8

Why, in the light of these obvious disadvantages, is payback so popular? The fact that it is easily calculated and easy to understand is in its favour. It is also, in a sense, a crude way of dealing with risk. Many managers would argue that the future is so uncertain that all cash flows after the first 2 or 3 years should be ignored. They would contend that if a project does not pay for itself within that length of time it is too risky to be undertaken. However, to give 100% weight to early cash flows and 0% weight to the cash flows which occur after a certain time period is clearly a very inexact approach to dealing with risk.

The accounting rate of return method is so named because it uses accounting numbers — not because it is the method which is universally adopted by accountants. The accounting rate of return can be defined in a number of different ways. Two of the most popular are

$$\frac{\text{Average profit per annum after tax from investment}}{\text{Initial Capital Outlay}}$$

and

$$\frac{\text{Average profit per annum after tax from investment}}{\text{Average book value of investment}}$$

Although this method (unlike payback period) considers the benefits from the project in all years, it takes no account of their timing. Net profits of £60,000 in year 1, £60,000 in year 2, £60,000 in year 3 and £60,000 in year 4 would be viewed in exactly the same way by the measure as net profits of £15,000 in year 1, £15,000 in year 2, £30,000 in year 3 and £180,000 in year 4 even though the former pattern is clearly preferable. The accounting rate of return also has the disadvantage referred to in the previous section that it considers accounting profits, not cash flows. The apparent attractiveness of a project using the method is always liable to depend critically on the depreciation method adopted by the company for the fixed assets in which it is considering investing.

Net Present Value (NPV) and Internal Rate of Return (IRR) are attempts to overcome the difficulties associated with simpler measures. The principle behind NPV is that if a company's minimum required rate of return is $r\%$ p.a. then the cash flow C_i received in i years time is equivalent to a cash flow

$$\frac{C_i}{\left(1 + \frac{r}{100}\right)^i}$$

received now. (This is because the latter cash flow, if invested at $r\%$ per annum, would grow to C_i by year i).

NPV values all cash flows in present-day terms, giving rise to the formula:

$$NPV = C_0 + \frac{C_1}{\left(1 + \frac{r}{100}\right)} + \frac{C_2}{\left(1 + \frac{r}{100}\right)^2} \cdots + \frac{C_n}{\left(1 + \frac{r}{100}\right)^n}$$

(Discount tables are available to simplify the calculation in this formula).

r, the minimum required rate of return, should be the company's opportunity cost of capital. In some situations it will correspond to the average return required by the providers of capital to the company; in other situations where capital is not readily available it will correspond to the return the company can get from alternative projects.

A NPV which is greater than zero is an indication that the investor is receiving greater than the minimum acceptable return ($r\%$ p.a.) on his funds. If it is negative, the reverse is true. The NPV itself represents the immediate increase in wealth to the firm arising from accepting the project. Assuming that capital can be raised freely at $r\%$ p.a. interest, it is the amount of money the firm could raise (in addition to any initial outlays) to distribute to the shareholders and, by the end of the project's life, have paid off all the capital and the interest.

The IRR is defined as that value of r which is such that:

$$C_0 + \frac{C_1}{1 + \frac{r}{100}} + \frac{C_2}{\left(1 + \frac{r}{100}\right)^2} \cdots + \frac{C_n}{\left(1 + \frac{r}{100}\right)^n} = 0. \qquad (1.1)$$

It represents the highest (net of tax) rate of interest at which the firm could afford to raise money for the project (providing of course that it has the option to repay the money whenever it chooses). The reason for this is indicated by Equation (1.1) which shows that the NPV is zero if money is raised at the internal rate of return rate of interest.

The definitions of NPV and IRR can be illustrated with the example in Table 2.

The net present value with a discount rate (r) of 10% per annum is (in £'000s).

$$- 160 + \frac{80}{1.1} + \frac{80}{1.1^2} + \frac{100}{1.1^3} + \frac{100}{1.1^4} = 122.28$$

TABLE 2. PROJECT USED FOR THE CALCULATION
OF NPV AND IRR

Year	Net cash flow (£'000s)
0	-160
1	80
2	80
3	100
4	100

With a discount rate of 20% p.a. this becomes 68.32 and with a discount of 30% per annum it is 29.41. The internal rate of return (which must be calculated by a systematic trial and error procedure) is 40.2%.

There has been a great deal of discussion in the literature of the relative advantages and disadvantages of NPV and IRR, and the reader who would like to pursue this particular aspect of capital budgeting further should consult references such as Merrett and Sykes (1963), Mao (1966), Teichrow et al. (1965) and Adelson (1970). It is now generally agreed that NPV is preferable to IRR. The main points which should be made when the two are being compared are:

(a) IRR is independent of the magnitudes of the cash flows, whereas NPV is not. In Table 1, projects B and D have the same IRR (approximately 35%) but the NPV of project B is ten times that of project D. For this reason, the way in which NPV and IRR rank alternative projects is not always the same: the IRR ranks projects according to the "breakeven cost of capital", and independently of the total sum of money invested; whereas the NPV ranks projects according to the increase in wealth which they bring to the company.

(b) If the investment is such that some cash flows after the initial one are negative (i.e. if it requires significant outlays of money at times other than the beginning of its life) then Equation (1.1) may have more than one solution and the IRR may become difficult to interpret. However, it is relatively rare for any real difficulties to be caused in this way. Situations where the initial investment is spread out over several years do not generally give rise to more than one solution. In other situations where an investment requires an additional periodical injection of cash, it is often easy to see that the total net cash flow stream can be split into several simpler ones, each with the same IRR (see Merrett and Sykes, 1963).

(c) It is dangerous to interpret the IRR in any natural way as the rate of return on the initial funds invested in a project during its life. The IRR is the return on the *declining balance* of the funds invested in a project. Consider the examples in Table 3 of two projects requiring the same initial investment. Project I has a higher IRR but a lower NPV (using a 5% discount rate) than project II. This is because, if we are talking about the return on £20,000 over a 2-year period, the IRR assumes that cash flows are reinvested at the IRR rate of interest, whereas NPV assumes that they are reinvested at 5%. In project I more funds have to be reinvested than in project II. The IRR can only be correctly interpreted as the maximum possible cost of capital if the company is not to make a loss on the project.

TABLE 3. PROJECTS WHICH ILLUSTRATE THE DIFFICULTIES LIABLE TO BE ENCOUNTERED IN INTERPRETING IRR

| | Cash flow | | | IRR (%) | NPV (discount rate = 5%) |
	Year 0	Year 1	Year 2		
Project I	−20,000	20,000	6,250	25	4,716
Project II	−20,000	4,000	24,000	20	5,578

1.4 The Discount Rate

The correct use of the NPV and IRR performance measures requires the specification of a company discount rate. In this case of NPV the discount rate is used in the calculation of the performance measure itself; in the case of IRR the discount rate is a standard against which the performance measure should be compared.

The discount rate, as mentioned before, should be the company's after-tax opportunity cost of capital. For a company which is not capital constrained, the opportunity cost of capital is simply the cost to the company of the capital it uses. When considering a project it is usually quite wrong to set the discount rate equal to the cost of the capital used to finance that particular project. The investment and financing decisions within a company should, as far as possible, be kept separate. A project should not be viewed favourably because, at the time it is being undertaken, the company happens to be using debt capital (which is a relatively cheap source of funds). If debt is being used this year, equity (a more expensive source of funds) will almost certainly have to be used next year if the company's debt:equity ratio is to be maintained within acceptable limits. A better procedure is to set the discount rate equal to the average cost of the funds which the company expects to use over the next few years. The funds should be viewed as going into a "pool" and being "mixed up" while individual projects dip into the pool for funds. The only exception to this rule arises when the finance for a project is inextricably tied to the project itself.

A company's capital comes from five main sources:

> debt
> preference shares
> new equity
> retained earnings
> depreciation.

The after-tax cost of debt is fairly straightforward. For example, if a company pays an interest rate of 10% p.a. on its debt capital, and pays tax at a marginal rate of 52% then the effective after-tax cost of the debt is 4.8% assuming there are no time lags between profits being earned and taxes being paid. The cost of preference capital is not calculated in quite the same way, because dividends on preference shares are not allowable against tax. In the UK at the time of writing one of the consequences of advanced corporation tax is that the net cost of preference shares to a company is 70% of their gross cost, assuming that the company has taxable income.

The cost of equity for a company can be defined as the rate of return which shareholders expect on the money which they have invested in the company. Generally, the riskier the company, the greater the returns which the shareholders expect. The cost of equity should rise as either the business risk or the financial risk of the company increases. Conceptually, the cost of new equity is no more difficult to determine than the cost of debt. It is the discount rate which makes the present value of the shareholders' expected future cash flows — dividends and sales price — equal to the present market value of his shares. If k is the cost of equity, D_i is the net dividend in year i, and P_i is the share price in year i, then

$$P_0 = \frac{D_1}{1 + k} + \frac{D_2}{(1 + k)^2} \cdots + \frac{D_{n-1}}{(1 + k)^{n-1}} + \frac{D_n + P_n}{(1 + k)^n}$$

In practice, the cost of equity capital is considerably more difficult to determine than the cost of debt capital because of the uncertainty surrounding the D_i and P_is. If it is assumed that:

(a) the company maintains a constant non-zero dividend yield; and
(b) dividends grow at rate g forever (and, therefore, from (a) the expected share price grows at rate g forever)

then is can be shown that the above equation reduces to

$$P_0 = \frac{D_1}{k - g}.$$

and, therefore, that

$$k = \frac{D_1}{P_0} + g.$$

It should be stressed that this formula is only appropriate when the conditions in (a) and (b) above hold (at least approximately). If the dividend yield is zero, or if it is expected to decline over time (e.g. because of statutory dividend constraints), the shareholder's expected capital gains must be considered carefully.

Another method for calculating the cost of equity involves relating the returns on an asset to its risk by means of the capital asset pricing model. This is dicussed in Chapter 7.

Retained earnings are not free to a company (as is sometimes assumed).

Retained earnings are funds which the directors have chosen to reinvest for the shareholder; and as such they have an opportunity cost approximately equal to the shareholder's required rate of return from the company. It can be argued that the cost of retained earnings and new equity are different because of their different tax treatments. If earnings are distributed to the shareholder as dividends he pays income tax on the dividends; if they are retained in the company he eventually pays capital gains tax on the resultant increase in share price.

Depreciation funds are usually regarded as having a cost equal to the average cost of all other sources. This is because the use of depreciation funds generally reduces the extent to which other funds are used in proportion to the total usage of those funds. Depreciation funds can, therefore, be ignored in the calculation of a company's average cost of capital.

Once the cost of the different sources of funds have been determined they should be weighted according to the extent to which they are expected to be used. For example, if a company expects to use 30% debt, 20% new equity, and 50% retained earnings, and these three sources of funds have costs of 10%, 16% and 15% respectively, the overall weighted average percentage cost of capital is $0.3 \times 10 + 0.2 \times 16 + 0.5 \times 15 = 13.7\%$.

The real problem in determining a company's cost of capital lies in getting a suitable value for the cost of equity. Any estimate of the minimum return which will satisfy shareholders is always liable to be subject to a wide margin of error.

The cost of capital calculated by the above process is a money cost of capital rather than a real cost of capital. It corresponds to a money rate of interest and describes the return which the providers of funds will receive, measured in £s of the years in which they receive those returns. As such, it is the discount rate which should be used in conjunction with money cash flows. The real cost of capital, C_R (which measures the return which the providers of funds get in today's £s), will, in times of inflation, be less than the money cost of capital, C_M, and an approximate formula for relating the two is $C_R = C_M - f$, where f is the rate of inflation. If all cash flows are expected to be subject to the same rate of inflation using real cash flows with a real discount rate will give the same NPV as using money cash flows with a money discount rate. In practice, however, not all cash flows are subject to the same rate of inflation. (Tax allowances on capital equipment, for example are not subject to inflation at all.) It is, therefore, sensible to apply the appropriate rate of inflation to each cash flow stream taken separately and then use a money discount rate.

1.5. Adjustments to the Discount Rate

Using the method described in the previous section, a company's average cost of capital is the overall expected return which the providers of funds to the company require. This average cost of capital should be modified when it is applied to individual projects.

Consider a project which, from the point of view of the providers of funds, is riskier than average (e.g. launching a new product in an unfamiliar market). If the company accepts the project then its overall riskiness increases. In order to satisfy the providers of funds (who require increased returns for increased risks), the company should use a discount rate (or in the case of IRR a criterion rate) which is rather greater than its average cost of capital. Similarly, it can use a discount rate which is rather less than its average cost of capital for projects with a lower than average risk, because such projects will tend to reduce the overall riskiness of the returns from the company.

The problem with this idea is that it may be difficult for management to assess the riskiness of a project without an analysis of the individual uncertainties, and of the way in which the uncertainties combine to form the overall project risk. Often it is necessary to adopt some fairly simple rules of thumb. For example, all cost-reduction projects might be classified as low risk, all plant expansion projects as medium risk, and all projects involving new products as high risk. Discount rates of 10%, 15% and 20% might then be assigned to these three types of projects respectively. However, these discount rates are not usually justified in any scientific way.

Sometimes a divisionalised company is able to recognise that certain divisions are in riskier lines of business than others. It can then set a different discount rate for each division. In theory, it is possible to set these discount rates scientifically. For each division, a publicly quoted company, which is solely in the same line of business as the division, must be found, and the discount rate for the division is calculated from the average cost of capital for the company. In practice, this is not as easy as it sounds. Very often it is simply not possible to find a publicly quoted company which is sufficiently similar to the division as far as its products and its markets are concerned.

A natural extension of the ideas which have been mentioned is to attempt a two-way classification — by type of project and by division — and to set up a matrix of discount rates. There is no objection to this provided that double counting is avoided. A division might be high risk simply because the projects it undertakes all involved new products.

The way in which the providers of funds would define the riskiness of a project is a topic which is taken up in Chapter 7. At this stage we merely note that some of the risks inherent in a project (or in the company as a whole) are not important to the providers of funds because they can be "diversified away". Other risks (e.g. those related to the performance of the economy as a whole) cannot be diversified away and are, therefore, of key importance.

It is usually true that a certain proportion of the projects undertaken by a company are not expected to generate any return. They might be undertaken to improve safety in the factory, provide recreational facilities for the workers, etc. The required rate of return on profit-orientated projects should be uplifted to allow for the fact that they have to "carry" these other projects. For example, if a company's average cost of capital is 7½%, and 25% of projects are not expected to generate any positive return, then the required rate of return on other projects should be raised to 10%.

It is worth noting that adjusting discount rates is not the only theoretically acceptable way of allowing for risk. Robichek and Myers (1965), and Cohen and Elton (1967) have suggested the use of certainty equivalents. Managements are asked to assess for each time period a cash flow which, if obtained for certain, is just as desirable as the projected uncertain cash flow. NPV and IRR are then calculated in the usual way. The chief disadvantage of the method is that the cash flow in any one time period is likely to be made up from several individual cash flows, each calculated from a number of different variables, and management may experience considerable difficulty in making the necessary assessments.

1.6.   Summary

This chapter has identified NPV and IRR as the two most acceptable measures of investment performance. NPV is the total present value of a project's future cash flows; IRR is the rate of return earned on the declining balance of funds tied up in the project.

Both NPV and IRR require the specification of a discount rate or cost of capital. The calculation of a company's average cost of capital involves knowing the cost of each source of capital taken separately. The cost of debt and preference share capital can be determined fairly precisely. Unfortunately, the cost of equity cannot readily be ascertained with any degree of precision because of the discretionary nature of dividends.

The average cost of capital is the discount rate which should be used for an average risk project. Projects which, from the point of view of providers of funds, have above average risks should use higher than average discount rates; while those with below average risks should use lower than average discount rates.

References

ADELSON, R. M. (1970). Discounted cash flow — can we discount it? A critical examination, *Journal of Business Finance,* vol. 2, no. 2, pp. 50–66.

COHEN, K. J. and ELTON, E. J. (1967). Inter-temporal portfolio analysis based on simulation of joint returns, *Management Science,* vol. 14, no. 1, pp. 5–18.

MAO, J. C. T. (1966). The internal rate of return as a ranking criterion, *Engineering Economist,* vol. 11, pp. 1–13.

MERRETT, A. J. and SYKES, A. (1963). *The finance and analysis of capital projects,* London, Longman.

ROBICHEK, A. A. and MYERS, S. C. (1965). *Optimal financing decisions,* Prentice Hall.

TEICHROW, D., ROBICHEK, A. A. and MONTALBANO, M. (1965). An analysis of criteria for investment and financing decisions under certainty, *Management Science,* vol. 12, no. 3, pp. 151–79.

Chapter 2
SOME PROCEDURES FOR QUANTIFYING RISK

2.1 Introduction

Estimates of the cash flows which would be generated by a proposed capital investment project in each year of its life are, almost invariably, built up from estimates of other variables. For example, in a project involving building a plant to manufacture a new product, the cash flows which are fed into the NPV calculation are likely to be calculated from estimates of such variables as the size of the market, the company's market share, variable operating costs, etc. The risk in an investment project arises, essentially, from management's uncertainty about these "primary" variables. This uncertainty gives rise to uncertainty about the cash flow estimates which, in turn, creates uncertainty as far as the calculated performance measure is concerned.

In this chapter, two analytic procedures for quantifying risk are presented. The first involves carrying out a sensitivity analysis; the second involves carrying out what is known as a risk simulation. The first identifies, in an approximate way, the contribution of each of the primary variables to the overall risk of the project; while the second is an attempt to obtain, directly, a measure of the overall risk.

2.2 Sensitivity Analysis

A sensitivity analysis is always a useful first step in evaluating the risks inherent in an investment opportunity. It involves first calculating a performance measure (usually NPV or IRR) on the basis of cash flows calculated from "most likely" (or "best") estimates of the primary

16

variables, and then observing the effect on the performance measure of changes in each of these most likely estimates. The basic idea is simple: if a change in an estimate has very little effect on the performance measure, then the investment decision is not likely to depend to any great extent on the accuracy of that estimate. On the other hand, if a change in the estimate produces a large change in the performance measure then the uncertainty surrounding the estimate may well be a significant consideration when the investment decision is being made. Thus a sensitivity analysis can be regarded as a way of quickly identifying those variables which contribute most to the risk of the investment.

To illustrate the basic idea of a sensitivity analysis, consider a company faced with the decision of whether to buy plant and machinery in order to enter a new market. We shall suppose that:

(i) there are only five uncertain variables — the company's market share, variable operating costs, fixed operating costs, advertising costs and the life of the plant and machinery;

(ii) the initial investment required is £200,000, the industry market size (measured in units sold p.a.) is 20M, the unit price is £0.60 and that these last two figures are expected to remain constant during the life of the investment;

(iii) taxation, working capital increases and all other variables can be ignored.

These assumptions, of course, are somewhat unrealistic. They have been chosen simply to make the example easier to follow.

Suppose that management's most likely estimates for the five variables are as shown in the second column of Table 4. On the basis of these estimates the net cash inflow in each year of the life of the investment can be shown to be £40,000, and the net present value, assuming a discount rate of 10% p.a., is £45,800. The third, fourth and fifth columns in Table 4 show the effect on net present value of a 10% change in the estimate made for a given variable, all other variables being kept fixed at their most likely values.

This is one way of carrying out a sensitivity analysis. It has the advantage that once the most likely estimates have been made the whole analysis can be performed fairly easily. However, it also has one very serious

TABLE 4. SENSITIVITY ANALYSIS BASED ON 10% ERRORS IN
EACH VARIABLE

Variable	Most likely estimate	10% change in most likely estimate	New value of NPV if 10% change (£'000s)	Decrease in NPV if 10% change (£'000s)
Percentage market share	10	9	−77.1	122.9
Variable operating cost per unit (£)	0.50	0.55	−568.7	614.5
Fixed operating cost p.a. (£)	100,000	110,000	−15.7	61.5
Advertising costs p.a. (£)	60,000	66,000	8.9	36.9
Life of plant and machinery (year)	10	9	30.4	15.4

disadvantage. The changes considered in the Table (10% of the most likely estimate) may not be directly comparable. For example, a 10% change in the market share estimate might be quite reasonable, whereas a 10% change in the operating costs estimate might be out of the question.

A natural alternative to Table 4 is Table 5. Here, in addition to supplying a most likely estimate for each variable, management have made an "optimistic" and "pessimistic" estimate. For each variable the Table shows:

(a) the values of the performance measure when the variable is equal to its optimistic estimate, all other variables being kept equal to their most likely values;

(b) the value of the performance measure when the variable is equal to its pessimistic estimate, all other variables being kept equal to their most likely values;

(c) the difference between (a) and (b).

The final column of Table 5 provides a set of numbers which are directly comparable. It shows that the uncertainty surrounding the advertising costs estimate is more important than the uncertainty of any other variable; that the uncertainty surrounding the fixed operating costs estimate is of negligible importance, and so on. This method of presentation is open to the objection that it requires managers to make more estimates than before. However, it is difficult to see how a Table such as Table 4 can be meaningfully interpreted without these extra estimates being made either explicitly or implicitly.

TABLE 5. SENSITIVITY ANALYSIS BASED ON OPTIMISTIC AND PESSIMISTIC ESTIMATES

Variable	Most likely estimate	Optimistic estimate	Pessimistic estimate	NPV if optimistic estimate (a)	NPV if pessimistic estimate (b)	Range of NPV (c)
Percentage market share	10	11.5	9.5	230.1	−138.6	368.7
Variable operating costs per unit (£)	0.50	0.49	0.52	168.7	−200	368.7
Fixed operating costs p.a. (£)	100,000	99,000	102,000	51.9	33.5	18.4
Advertising costs p.a. (£)	60,000	20,000	100,000	291.6	−200	491.6
Life of plant and machinery	10	15	5	104.2	−48.4	152.6

The definitions of the terms "optimistic estimate" and "pessimistic estimate" deserve some consideration. It is not necessary for the optimistic estimate to be the "best conceivable" value for the variable and for the pessimistic estimate to be the "worst conceivable" value. It is, however, necessary to be consistent in the use of the terms. Some rules such as: "there should be a 5% chance of the value of the variable being greater than the optimistic estimate, and a 5% chance of it being less than the pessimistic estimate" should be chosen. There are problems in getting managers to think in terms of probabilistic estimates. These will be dealt with in the next chapter.

2.3 The Limitations of Sensitivity Analysis

In a sensitivity analysis it is customary to consider only one error in one variable at a time (For this reason, when errors in the market share estimate were considered in Tables 4 and 5 all other variables were held fixed at their most likely estimates, etc.) The effects on the performance measure of combinations of errors in different variables is, therefore, largely ignored by a sensitivity analysis. (Some interesting developments concerning the use of a sensitivity analysis to estimate the total risk in an investment will be discussed in Chapter 5.)

In a sensitivity analysis it is often tempting to:

(a) calculate a performance measure by combining together all the pessimistic estimates;

(b) calculate a performance measure by combining together all the optimistic estimates,

and then to use the difference between the two as a measure of the investment's risk. This would not be very meaningful as the assumption implicit in (a) that each variable equals its pessimistic estimate is unreasonably over-pessimistic and, similarly, the assumption implicit in (b) is unreasonably over-optimistic. To emphasise this point; suppose that each of five independent variables has a 5% chance (i.e. 1 chance in 20) of being worse than its pessimistic estimate. The chance of every single one of the variables being worse than its pessimistic estimate is less than one in a million. (Note that although this illustrates an idea it somewhat overstates the case. In order to get a value of the performance measure below the value which is obtained by combining pessimistic estimates it is not necessary for each value of each variable to be worse than its pessimistic estimate. One variable which is slightly better than its pessimistic estimate may be combined with another which is considerably worse, etc.)

In spite of this, it is still worth carrying out the calculations in (a) and (b) above. If the investment is unacceptable when optimistic estimates are combined together, it is almost certainly not worth considering further. If it is acceptable when pessimistic estimates are combined together, it can usually be accepted without further analysis.

A methodological difficulty with sensitivity analyses arises when there is a dependence between two variables. Dependence is an important concept in risk analysis and one which will be returned to in Chapter 4. Briefly, two variables are dependent if a knowledge of the value of one would influence the estimates made for the other. Two situations are possible:

(i) positive dependence: where it is considered that if one variable has a high value, the other variable will probably have a high value (and where if one variable has a low value then so will the other variable);

(ii) negative dependence: where it is considered that if one variable has a high value the other will probably have a low value.

Dependencies cause difficulties in a sensitivity analysis because when they are present it is not strictly correct to consider errors in only one variable at a time. To take an example; suppose that the home market and the export market for a certain product are considered to be positively dependent in a certain situation (i.e. it is considered that if the home market is above its most likely estimate, then the export market will also be above its most likely estimate, etc.). Then, when an error is being considered in the home market, the original most likely estimate for the export market is no longer strictly appropriate. In such practical situations the analyst has two choices:

(a) ignore the dependence and proceed as described in the previous section; or,

(b) assume total dependence and whenever a certain error is considered in one of the variables, automatically consider a corresponding error in the other variable.

Neither of these two alternatives is altogether satisfactory. Which one is chosen in a particular situation will depend on a judgement as to the strength of the dependence.

2.4 Probability Distributions and Risk Profiles

"Pessimistic" and "optimistic" estimates provide an indication of the uncertainty surrounding the best estimate made for a particular variable but, for a complete description of that uncertainty, a probability distribution is required. Briefly, a probability distribution describes how probability is distributed over the range of possible values of a variable. It is a curve which provides a good visual indication of the relative likelihoods of different values of the variable occurring. A possible probability distribution for the variable market share has been drawn in Fig. I. It shows that the most likely market share is 10%, that a market share of 11% is about a quarter as likely as 10%, etc.

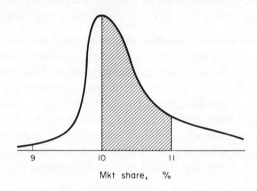

9   10   11

Mkt share,   %

FIG. I.   A possible probability distribution for the variable market share.

A rigorous definition of a probability distribution would be as follows:

A probability distribution is a curve such that the area under the curve between two points is equal to the probability of the variable lying between those two points.

Thus the shaded area in Fig. I represents the probability of the market share lying between 10% and 11%.

Sometimes probability distributions can be based on past data. However, when major capital investment opportunities are being analysed the situation is usually completely different from any previously encountered by the company and no data are available. Probability distributions which are subjective (i.e. based on managerial judgement rather than data) must then be used. A full discussion of subjective probability distributions and the way in which they can be obtained is contained in Chapter 3.

One way of describing an investment's risk is by means of a probability distribution of its performance measure and this is sometimes referred to as its "risk profile". Figure II provides an example of a probability distribution of NPV and Fig. III shows the corresponding cumulative distribution. From the latter any probabilities likely to be of interest can be picked out. For example, Fig. III shows that the probability of NPV being negative is approximately 0.1, that the probability of NPV being greater than £20M is approximately 0.2, etc.

Much of the work which has been carried out in the area of risk evaluation has been concerned with deriving Figures such as Fig. II and Fig. III from the distributions of uncertain variables. One interesting point to note is that in addition to supplying information about risk such analysis

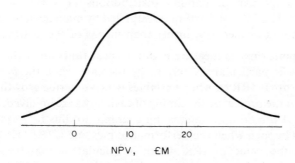

FIG. II.   Probability distribution for NPV.

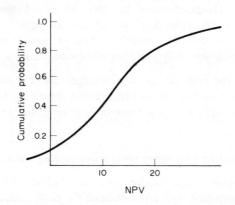

FIG. III.   Cumulative probability distribution for NPV.

often improves upon estimates of the mean or expected return from an investment. This is because there is often a discrepancy between:

(a) the value of the performance measure which is calculated from management's best (i.e. most likely) estimates; and

(b) the mean of the distribution of the performance measure.

This discrepancy will not generally arise if the performance measure is a linear function of the variables and the best estimates made by management for the variables correspond to their means. It is, however, liable to occur if:

(i) the subjective probability distributions of some variables are skewed and the best estimates supplied by management correspond to modes or medians, rather than means of the distributions;

(ii) the performance measure is not a linear function of the variables. (This is particularly likely to be the case when the performance measure is IRR or when variables which describe growth rates, the life of the project or the timing of cash flows are involved. Robichek (1975) provides an interesting example to illustrate exactly what does happen when the performance measure is IRR. He concludes that the value of IRR which is calculated from the means of variables will tend to be greater than the mean of IRR);

(iii) there are dependencies between the subjective probabilities of the variables. (Dependencies between variables which are added together in the cash-flow model do not cause problems, but a dependency between variables, such as market size and market share, which are multiplied together does cause a discrepancy.)

In some cases the discrepancy is quite large. In a case study discussed in Hertz (1964) the expected value of the rate of return is 14.6% whereas the rate of return calculated on the basis of best estimates is 25.2%.

2.5 Analytic approaches towards determining a risk profile

As far as analytic approaches to the problem of determining a probability distribution for an investment's performance measure are concerned, Hillier (1963, 1969) and Wagle (1967) have made significant contributions. The work of these authors is, for the most part, concerned with calculating the mean and standard deviation of NPV from the means and standard deviations of, and the co-efficients of correlation between, the variables. This section will describe some of their results.

If the net cash flow C_i in year i is considered to have a mean of μ_i and a standard deviation of σ_i then, assuming the cash flows in different years are independent of each other, the mean of NPV is

$$\sum_{i=0}^{n} \frac{\mu_i}{\left(1 + \frac{r}{100}\right)^i} \qquad (2.1)$$

and the variance of NPV is

$$\sum_{i=0}^{n} \frac{\sigma_i^2}{\left(1 + \frac{r}{100}\right)^{2i}} \qquad (2.2)$$

If different cash flows are dependent with ρ_{ij} being the coefficient of correlation between C_i and C_j, then the formula for the mean of NPV remains unchanged while the variance of NPV becomes

$$\sum_{i=0}^{n} \frac{\sigma_i^2}{\left(1 + \frac{r}{100}\right)^{2i}} + \sum_{i \neq j} \frac{\sigma_i \, \sigma_j \, \rho_{ij}}{\left(1 + \frac{r}{100}\right)^{i+j}}$$

If it is possible for management to make estimates of the net cash flows directly then the above formulae can, in principle, be used as they stand. When net cash flows have to be calculated from the values of other variables Wagle (1967) shows that it is possible to use standard statistical results concerned with the means and standard deviations of the sums and products of variables. Suppose that variables X_1 and X_2 have means m_1 and m_2 and standard deviations s_1 and s_2 and that a_1 and a_2 are constants. Then:

(i) if X_1 and X_2 are independent

Mean of $(a_1 X_1 + a_2 X_2)$ $= a_1 m_1 + a_2 m_2$ (2.3)
Variance of $(a_1 X_1 + a_2 X_2) = a_1^2 s_1^2 + a_2^2 s_2^2$ (2.4)
Mean of $X_1 X_2$ $= m_1 m_2$ (2.5)
Variance of $X_1 X_2$ $= m_1^2 s_2^2 + m_2^2 s_1^2 + s_1^2 s_2^2$; (2.6)

(ii) if X_1 and X_2 are dependent with coefficient of correlation ρ

Mean of $(a_1 X_1 + a_2 X_2)$ $= a_1 m_1 + a_2 m_2$ (2.7)
Variance of $(a_1 X_1 + a_2 X_2) = a_1^2 s_1^2 + a_2^2 s_2^2 + 2 \rho a_1 a_2 s_1 s_2$ (2.8)
Mean of $X_1 X_2$ $= m_1 m_2 + \rho s_1 s_2$ (2.9)
(Formula for variance of $X_1 X_2$ is complex.)

As a simple illustration of the use of the above results; suppose that in a certain new product launch situation there are three uncertain variables

Fixed costs   F
Variable costs V
Market size   M

with the means and standard deviation indicated in Table 6. Suppose that F, M and V are independent of each other in all 3 years and that the value of any one of the variables in one year is independent of its value in another year.

TABLE 6. DATA FOR EXAMPLE ILLUSTRATING THE ANALYTIC
APPROACH TO RISK EVALUATION

	Mean	Standard deviation
F = Fixed costs (£ p.a.)	5000	1000
V = Variable costs (£ per unit)	2	0.5
M = Market size p.a. (units)	10,000	1000

We shall assume that the product will last 5 years, that the initial investment required is £10,000, that its price is £3 per unit and that complications such as tax and working capital can be ignored.

During years 1–5 the net cash flow is

$$M (3 - V) - F.$$

The variable

$$3 - V$$

has mean 1 and standard deviation 0.5. The variable

$$M (3 - V)$$

has from Equations (2.5) and (2.6) a mean of 10,000 and a standard deviation of

$$\sqrt{(1^2 \times 1000^2 + 10,000^2 \times 0.5^2 + 0.5^2 \times 1000^2)}$$
$$= 5123$$

The variable

$$M (3 - V) - F$$

has, using the results in Equations (2.3) and (2.4), a mean of

$$10,000 - 5000 = 5000$$

and a standard deviation of

$$\sqrt{(5123^2 + 1000^2)}$$
$$= 5220$$

Using the results in Equations (2.1) and (2.2), the mean of NPV is, if we assume a discount rate of 10% p.a.,

$$- 10,000 + \sum_{i=1}^{5} \frac{5000}{1.1^i}$$
$$= 8954$$

and the variance of NPV (assuming perhaps unrealistically that the cash flows are independent) is

$$\sum_{i=1}^{5} \frac{5220^2}{1.1^{2i}}$$
$$= 79,728,000$$

giving a standard deviation for NPV of 8929.

It should be emphasised that, in situations where the analytic approach can be used, the calculations are usually more complicated than those given above because it is not reasonable to assume that the value of a variable in one year is independent of its value in the previous year.

Analytic approaches generally have the disadvantage that they provide a mean and standard deviation for NPV rather than a complete probability distribution. Hillier (1963, 1969) presents a number of theoretical arguments which strongly suggest that the distribution of NPV is often, in practice, approximately normal so that the mean and standard deviation are all that is required. The author's own experience with risk evaluation (see Hull, 1977) leads him to conclude that NPV is likely to be normal in investment situations except when:

(a) the investor has options (e.g. abandonment or expansion options) open to him at stages during the project's life;

(b) the distribution of NPV is heavily influenced by non-linearities in the cash flow model; and

(c) there is a small number of uncertain variables, or the uncertainty in one variable dominates all other uncertainties.

It is worth noting that if the distribution of NPV is approximately normal, and if the analyst is prepared to calculate its mean and standard deviation for a number of different discount rates, then the distribution of IRR can be calculated using the relationships:

Prob. (IRR $< d$) = Prob. (NPV < 0 when discount rate is d).

Analytic approaches to the problem of evaluating risk are considered further in Chapter 5.

2.6 Sampling from a Probability Distribution and Risk Simulation

One important concept in risk simulation is that of a random sample from a probability distribution. Briefly, a sample is random if all values in the range of possible values have a chance of being selected, and the relative chances of different values being selected is determined by the probability distribution of the variable.

Taking a random sample from a distribution which is based on data is theoretically straightforward. Each data item is written on a separate slip of paper, all the slips of paper are put in a hat and after the hat has been shaken one is selected. Taking a random sample from a subjective probability distribution such as that shown in Fig. I is not quite so simple. In theory, it is possible to:

(a) divide the distribution into a number of intervals calculating the probability of the variable lying in each interval;

(b) manufacture data for the distribution on the basis of the probabilities calculated in (a) (e.g. if there is a 0.15 probability of the variable lying in a particular interval ensure that this fraction of the data does so, etc.);

(c) proceed as indicated above for a distribution based on past data.

In practice, it is often necessary in risk simulation to sample hundreds or even thousands of times from probability distributions and a computer procedure must be used. The precise details of such computer procedures need not concern us at this stage.

Risk simulation provides an alternative to the analytic approaches to risk evaluation which were considered in Section 2.5. The basic procedure is illustrated in Fig. IV. Probability distributions for the variables must be obtained either on the basis of past data or subjectively using the methods to be discussed in the next chapter. Each of the distributions is then sampled from once. This provides a single value for each of the variables and enables a set of net cash flows and, therefore, a value for the performance measure, to be calculated. (This value for the performance measure can be regarded as a random sample from the distribution of the performance measure.) The distributions are then sampled from again and a new value for the performance measure is calculated, and so on. Eventually, after a large number of samplings from the distributions (say 500) enough different values for the performance measure are obtained for a probability distribution of the performance measure to be drawn.

The calculations in risk simulation are almost invariably carried out by a computer and Appendix B provides a set of subroutines which could be used by the reader.

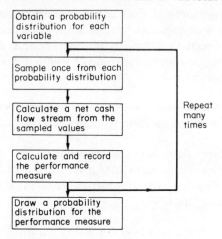

FIG. IV.   The risk simulation methodology.

A detailed discussion of all aspects of risk simulation is contained in the chapters which follow. At this stage two points are worthy of note:

(*a*) A sensitivity analysis should always be carried out prior to a risk simulation in order to determine the relative importance of different variables. If a variable is found to be very important, a great deal of care should be taken in arriving at its distribution. On the other hand, if the sensitivity analysis indicates that the precise value of the variable makes very little difference to the performance measure it is probably not worth assigning a distribution to the variable at all. Using the same value for the variable in all calculations should, in such cases, be sufficient. (This point will be discussed further in Chapter 5.)

(*b*) Dependencies can be handled within a risk simulation in a number of different ways. Hertz (1964), who is one of the originators of the simulation approach, suggests that a single subjective probability distribution be assessed for the independent variable and that several subjective probability distributions be assessed for the dependent variable, each one being conditional on the independent variable lying in a certain interval. On each run of the simulation the value sampled for the independent variable then determines the particular conditional subjective probability distribution used. This illustrates the principle, but has the disadvantage that management are asked to make a very large number of individual probability judgements. Simplifying assumptions often have to be made in practice and this aspect of risk simulation is discussed in Chapter 4.

Many applications of risk simulation have been published in the literature. Pouliquen (1970) in a first-rate publication describes in detail several applications of the technique to the investment proposals facing the World Bank. Economos (1968) describes how risk simulation was used to determine whether a company should enter the computer leasing business. Kryzanowski *et al.* (1972) and Bussey and Stevens (1972) use risk simulation to deal with proposed plant expansions. Fowkes (1971) describes its application to branch bank location decisions.Smith (1970) and Newendorp and Root (1968) are concerned with its application to petroleum investment decisions. Cameron (1972) shows how it can be used in the case of a proposal to invest in thirty-four hotels. Other applications are provided by Glasgall (1968), Brown (1970) and Richards and Contesse (1975). Finally, the problems of introducing risk simulation into an organisation are considered by Carter (1972), Hall (1975) and Longbottom and Wade (1971).

The sample size in a risk simulation is, in practice, often chosen by trial and error. Sometimes two separate simulations with different random number streams but the same number of runs are carried out and, if the results are sufficiently close, the number of runs is deemed to be adequate. As a general guide, if μ_p is the mean of the performance measure and σ_p is its standard deviation the standard error of μ_p is

$$\frac{\sigma_p}{\sqrt{n}}$$

and the standard error of σ_p is:

$$\frac{\sigma_p}{\sqrt{2n}}$$

2.7 Comparison of Analytic and Simulation Approaches

Simulation approaches to risk evaluation are, at the present time, far more popular than analytic approaches. The chief disadvantage of the simulation approach was, at one time, the cost of the computer time used. However, technological developments have now reduced the costs of running even a large risk simulation model to negligible proportions. The chief computing costs are usually those incurred in connection with the development of subroutines for carrying out the cash flow calculations.

The major advantage of the simulation approach is that there are virtually no restrictions as far as the complexity of the model which relates cash flows to other variables is concerned. An analytic approach becomes very difficult, and sometimes impossible, when:

(i) there are options (e.g. abandonment or expansion options) open to the investor at stages during the project's life; or

(ii) non-linear variables such as "sales growth rate" and "life of project" are involved; or

(iii) there are dependencies between non-linear variables.

It must be emphasised at this stage that a company should never jump straight into using either of the two methods for producing risk profiles which have been described. A sensitivity analysis should always be carried out first. Very often, when full use is made of the ideas in Chapter 5, this is all that is required.

2.8 Risk Evaluation and Modern Financial Management Theory

According to modern financial management theory, capital investment projects must be considered from the point of view of the company's shareholders. The value to the shareholder of a risky cash flow in year n depends on the extent to which he can diversify away the risks by buying other securities, etc. This aspect of risk evaluation will be discussed in Chapter 7. The reader should appreciate at this stage that the techniques presented in this chapter are open to criticism because they are concerned with the total risk of an investment — not its marginal effect on a well-diversified shareholder.

Another related theoretical problem concerns the precise meaning of a distribution for NPV. In particular, what discount rate should be used? It would seem incorrect to use a risk-adjusted discount rate (see Section 1.5) as a risk profile is essentially concerned with measuring risk. To quote Myers (1976):

"If NPV is calculated using an appropriate risk adjusted discount rate, any further adjustment for risk is double-counting. If a risk free rate of interest is used instead then one obtains a distribution of what the project's value would be tomorrow if all uncertainty about the project's cash flows were resolved between today and tomorrow. But since uncertainty is not resolved in this way the meaning of the distribution is unclear."

These two criticisms are not easy to answer on a theoretical level. In a sense they are criticisms of sensitivity analyses and the interpretation of their output just as much as they are criticisms of risk profiles.

However, in spite of theoretical developments many companies are still interested in evaluating total investment risk — at least as a first step in their risk evaluation procedures. Furthermore, the choice of a discount rate does not present major problems in practice. Companies are usually interested in answers to questions such as:

"What is the chance that the project will provide a $Y\%$ return."

If $Y\%$ is used as the discount rate, the answer to this question is simply the probability of NPV being greater than zero. In many respects a distribution for IRR is more useful than one for NPV in answering questions such as the above.

2.9 Summary

This chapter has developed a number of ideas concerned with the quantification of risk in major capital investment decisions. It has argued that if a business requires a measure of the risk associated with a certain investment decision single most likely estimates for each of the variables are not enough. Management must also provide (as an indication of the range of possible values which each variable might take) "optimistic" and "pessimistic" estimates.

A sensitivity analysis provides a useful first step in any analysis of the riskiness of an investment. It involves (if the procedure recommended in this chapter is followed) taking each of the variables in turn and examining the effect on the performance measure of varying the value of the variable between its pessimistic and its optimistic estimate. The variables can then be ranked in a clear way according to their importance as contributors to the overall investment risk. The next step can then be the production of a risk profile for the investment. Two main approaches are available — the analytic approach and the simulation approach. The simulation approach involves assigning a probability distribution (either subjectively or on the basis of past data) to each of the variables identified as important contributors to the overall investment risk. Sampling once from the distributions enables a single value for the performance measure to be calculated. Repeated sampling enables a complete probability distribution for the measure to be obtained.

A risk profile does not definitely answer the question: Should the investment be accepted or rejected? This would be impossible. An investment which is considered to be acceptable to a large organisation might well be considered too risky by a small one, etc. A risk simulation does however provide a considerable increase in a company's understanding of how different factors interact to form the total risk in the project.

References

BROWN, G. A. (1970). The evaluation of risk in mining ventures, *Canadian Mining and Metallurgist Bulletin,* Oct., pp. 1165–71.

BUSSEY, L. E. and STEVENS, G. T. (1972). Formulating correlated cash flow streams, *Engineering Economist,* vol. 18, no. 1, pp. 1–30.

CAMERON. D. A. (1972). Risk analysis and investment appraisal in marketing, *Long Range Planning,* Dec., pp. 43–7.

CARTER, E. E. (1972). What are the risks in risk analysis, *Harvard Business Review,* July–Aug., pp. 72–82.

ECONOMOS, A. M. (1968). A financial simulation for risk analysis of a proposed subsidiary, *Management Science,* vol. 15, B, no. 12, pp. 675–82.

FOWKES, T. R. (1971). *Branch network planning for commercial banks.* PhD Thesis, University of London.

GLASGALL, P. T. (1968). *Probability — an application to projected airline cash flow,* Douglas Aircraft Company Paper No. 5052, May.

HALL, W. K. (1975). Why risk analysis isn't working, *Long Range Planning,* Dec., pp. 25–29.

HERTZ, D. B. (1964). Risk analysis in Capital Investment, *Harvard Business Review,* Jan–Feb., pp. 95–106.

HILLIER, F. S. (1963). The derivation of probabilistic information for the evaluation of risky investments, *Management Science*, vol. 9, no. 3, pp. 443–57.

HILLIER, F. S. (1969). *The evaluation of risky interrelated investments*, North-Holland.

HULL, J. C. (1977). The input to and output from risk evaluation models, *European Journal of Operational Research*, vol. 1, pp. 368–75.

KRYZANOWSKI, L., LUSZTIG, P. and SCHWAB, B. (1972). Monte Carlo simulation and capital expenditure decisions — a case study, *Engineering Economist*, vol. 18, no. 1, pp. 31–47.

LONGBOTTOM, D. A. and WADE, G. (1971). *The application of decision analysis in United Kingdom companies*, Durham University Business School Research Paper No. 1.

MYERS, S. C. (1976). Postscript: using simulation for Risk Analysis, in *Modern Developments in Financial Management*, edited by S. C. Myers, Holt Rinehart & Winston.

NEWENDORP, P. D. and ROOT, P. J. (1968). Risk analysis in drilling investment decisions, *Journal of Petroleum Technology*, June, pp. 579–85.

POULIQUEN, L. Y. (1970). *Risk analysis in project appraisal*, Johns Hopkins Press for the International Bank for Reconstruction and Development.

RICHARDS, P. and CONTESSE, A. (1975). Risk analysis in the North Sea, *The Investment Analyst*, no. 41, pp. 20–5.

ROBICHEK, A. A. (1975). Interpreting the results of risk analysis, *Journal of Finance*, vol. 30, no. 5, pp. 1384–6.

SMITH, M. B. (1970). Probability models for petroleum investment decisions, *Journal of Technology*, May, pp. 543–50.

WAGLE, B. (1967). A statistical analysis of risk in capital investment projects, *Operational Research Quarterly*, vol. 18, no. 1, pp. 13–33.

Chapter 3

FORECASTING AND THE ASSESSMENT OF SUBJECTIVE PROBABILITY DISTRIBUTIONS

3.1 Introduction

The most important stage in the evaluation of an investment opportunity is undoubtedly the stage during which estimates are made for the uncertain variables. If the estimates are well-thought-out and unbiased, the analytic procedures described so far can give a considerable insight into the viability of the investment. Unfortunately, it is all too often the case that estimates are hastily prepared and totally unrealistic. This leads to a situation where subsequent analysis is almost a complete waste of time.

This chapter is concerned with examining the different ways in which estimates — particularly probabilistic estimates — can be made. When reading the chapter it should be borne in mind that the amount of time which is spent on making estimates for a variable should be related in some way to the importance of that variable. This aspect of risk evaluation has already been touched upon; it will be discussed further in Chapter 5.

3.2 Making Estimates — Basic Approaches

There are three basic approaches to making estimates about the future. These can be summarised as:

    A. The use of historical data.
    B. The use of the judgement and experience of one person.
    C. The use of the judgement and experience of several people.

In this section we shall explore the relative advantages and disadvantages of each of the approaches and mention some of the reasons why the estimates they produce are liable to be biased. Later in the chapter a number of different procedures for making probabilistic estimates will be considered in detail and the whole subject of biases in estimation will be given more attention.

First let us consider approach A. A simple example of this approach in action would be the following statement:

"Over the last 5 years our UK market size has increased at 10% p.a. in real terms. Let us assume that this rate of increase will continue in the future."

The basic assumption in this and other similar statements is that a trend which has been observed in the past will continue in the future. This assumption is often quite reasonable when forecasting for a year or two ahead. However, when forecasts are being prepared for longer periods of time (as it usually the case in major capital investment-decision situations) it is of doubtful validity. The reason for this is often quite apparent when particular variables are considered. The author is reminded of a student who projected a 20% p.ą. growth rate in traffic flows on a certain road 50 years into the future without ever realising that it implied cars travelling literally bumper to bumper at 200 miles per hour for 24 hours per day!

An alternative to simple extrapolation when forecasting market size involves fitting past data to a "product life-cycle curve". This idea is discussed in Chambers et al. (1971). The product life-cycle (see Fig. V) represents the pattern which is often observed for the growth in the sales of a product over time. During early market testing and introduction, growth is slow but once the product is established a period of rapid growth follows. This in time is followed by a steady state situation. Bass (1969) has analysed data for eleven consumer durable products and shown that this model gives a good fit.

Another approach to making estimates by analysing past data involves relating the variable of interest to other variables using regression analysis. This can be successful but it should be borne in mind that the procedure is only of practical use if the new variables are easier to forecast than the original variable. The ideal relationship is a lagged relationship, when the value of the variable of interest is related to the values of other variables in a preceding time period. The relevant values of the other variables may then be known with certainty when the forecast is being produced.

Historical data is not always available on the key variables in a major

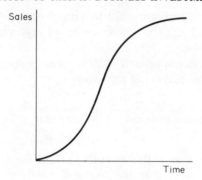

FIG. V.   The product life-cycle curve.

capital investment decision. When it is available it has the advantage that it is completely objective; two different people applying the same analytic procedures to the same data will always come up with the same answer. There is, however, the danger that too much reliance will be placed on the data and that the expert opinion which is available within the company will be ignored. It is all too often the case that just for the sake of having something "objective" to hang their arguments on, companies use data from previous situations which are not really relevant to the situation under consideration.

Moving on to the second of the three approaches mentioned at the beginning of this section, it is nothing like as easy to categorise the different ways in which a manager can use his experience to make estimates, as it is to describe the different ways in which data can be analysed. Most managers, when making subjective estimates, attempt to draw a parallel between the situation currently facing them and situations which they have previously encountered either directly or indirectly. This is what "using one's experience" is all about. Some people are better than others at using their experience. This is not necessarily because their experience is of a higher quality; it is sometimes a result of the flexibility they display in using that experience. Many readers will be familiar with managers who preface a large number of their remarks with "When I was at . . .". This is probably a sign of inflexibility.

Generally it can be said that experience should always be combined with a sound appreciation of the environmental factors affecting a company. Hussey (1974) provides a useful reference here. He distinguishes six different categories of environmental factors (demographic, economic, legal, technological, ecological and sociological) and he provides a good discussion of the nature of their influences on the company.

Probably the most difficult task for a manager when he is asked to make a subjective estimate is that of distinguishing between what he wants to happen and what he actually thinks will happen. If a manager is personally involved with a project he will naturally want that project to be a success and unless he is careful this is liable to make him less objective than he would otherwise be.

Another problem which companies frequently encounter when using approach B is concerned with the motivation of individual managers. If the estimates which are made by a manager are also used as yardsticks against which his performance is measured then there will be a natural tendency for the manager to be conservative. Ideally, the reward structure for an individual manager should be independent of any estimates which the manager has made.

We now move on to a consideration of the last of the three approaches outlined at the beginning of this section — namely, that of using judgement of a group of individuals rather than a single individual. It can be argued that this is a way of overcoming the biases which have just been mentioned. Not all the individuals will be heavily committed to the project and their reward structures will be different. The problem which immediately arises is that of combining a number of different estimates into a single estimate. Should a straight average be taken or should more weight be given to the estimates of more knowledgeable estimators? If there is group discussion to resolve any difference then there is a danger that the group will be unduly influenced by one or two dominant personalities.

One approach to group forecasting which has received a great deal of acclaim in the literature involves the use of what is known as the Delphi technique. This provides a way in which feedback can be incorporated into the estimating process. It involves interrogating managers by means of a sequence of questionnaires. The first questionnaire asks each manager to make, independently of the other managers, a number of estimates connected with the variable under consideration. These estimates are then put together and a summary of them is presented to each manager. The second questionnaire then asks each manager if, in the light of the judgements made by other managers, he would like to change his original estimates and the whole process is repeated again. The technique avoids any chance of the group being dominated by forceful personalities as the questionnaires are handled in an anonymous way. Accounts of experimental work involving the use of the technique are provided in Brown and Helmar (1962), Dalkey and Helmar (1963) and Moore and Thomas (1975).

3.3 Estimating Uncertainty

So far in this chapter the discussion has centred around the production of a single estimate for a variable. As will be readily appreciated from the arguments put forward in Chapter 2, single estimates are of limited usefulness. There is little value in knowing that a manager estimates £2M for turnover next year if it is also true that, in his opinion, the figure could reasonably be anywhere between £1.2M and £2.8M.

Apart from enabling a more meaningful analysis to be carried out, estimating uncertainty — either by the specification of pessimistic and optimistic estimates or by the assessment of a subjective probability distribution — can have other advantages. Once the basic procedures have been explained, managers are often far more willing to make uncertainty estimates than they are to make single point estimates for a variable. The reason for this is the personal commitment which is inherent in a point estimate. Woods (1966) provides a good discussion of this aspect of risk evaluation.

Most of the rest of this chapter will be devoted to a discussion of the procedures which are available for the assessment of subjective probability distributions. If the objective is to carry out a sensitivity analysis, the analyst is only likely to be interested in obtaining meaningful optimistic and pessimistic estimates for the variables. However, it should be noted that many of the biases which are liable to occur and the methods for overcoming them are broadly the same, whether one is talking about the assessment of extreme fractiles of a distribution or the assessment of the complete probability distribution. The particular problems associated with obtaining optimistic and pessimistic estimates will be discussed in Section 3.9.

3.4 The Validity of Subjective Probability Distributions

It will be useful to start our discussion of subjective probability distributions by considering the general objections which are sometimes raised against the use of subjective probabilities.

It is frequently argued:

(a) that subjective probabilities do not really exist in any meaningful sense;

(b) that subjective probabilities do not necessarily obey the additive and multiplicative rules of probability; and

(c) that subjective probabilities are less reliable than frequency probabilities.

To consider (a) let us take as an example a probability which, if it exists, is certainly subjective: the probability of a manned landing on Mars by the year AD 2000. A good way to convince someone that his probability really does exist is by asking him the following question:

> An urn contains 50 red balls and 50 black balls. Which would you rather bet on: a red ball being drawn from the urn or a manned landing on Mars by the year AD 2000.

If the answer is: "a red ball being drawn" reduce the proportion of red balls and ask the question again: if the answer is: "a manned landing on Mars" increase the proportion and ask the question again. Eventually, by continuing to compare the unknown subjective probability with different known frequency probabilities you should be able to determine his value for the subjective probability reasonably accurately. Of course there is no reason why two different people should make the same subjective probability estimate for a manned landing on Mars by AD 2000 (or indeed for any other uncertain event). In this sense, subjective probabilities are different from frequency-based probabilities and it is important that when subjective probabilities are used in practice they are assessed by those managers with most knowledge and experience.

As far as (*b*) is concerned, it is certainly true that the subjective probabilities which are assessed may not obey the rules of probability. For example, a manager without realising he was being inconsistent might make the following estimates while assessing a subjective probability distribution.

(i) Probability of sales being between 20M and 22M is 0.2
(ii) Probability of sales being between 22M and 24M is 0.25.
(iii) Probability of sales being between 20M and 24M is 0.5.

However, it has been shown that if the subjective probabilities which are assessed by an individual in a given situation do not obey the rules of probability, then it is possible to devise a series of bets such that the decisions taken by the individual will cause him to lose money whatever the outcome. It is therefore reasonable to conclude that most of us would like to be consistent in the probability assessments we make, and that if inconsistencies are pointed out to us we will take steps to iron them out.

(*c*) is usually motivated by feelings such as: "even if my subjective probability for a manned landing on Mars by AD 2000 were 0.5 I would still far rather bet on a coin coming up heads when tossed than on a manned landing on Mars because in the case of the coin the probabilities are certain". Our natural inclinations are to prefer probabilities based on a great deal of information rather than ones based on relatively little information. These natural inclinations, however, must sometimes be curbed as they are liable to lead to inconsistencies. Consider two urns: Urn A contains 50 red balls and 50 black balls; urn B contains 100 red and black balls but in an unknown proportion. Your natural inclinations would probably be:

(i) to prefer betting on a red ball being drawn from urn A rather than betting on a red ball being drawn from urn B;

(ii) to prefer betting on a black ball being drawn from urn A rather than betting on a black ball being drawn from urn B;

even though this can easily be shown to be inconsistent, as the sum of the probability of drawing a red ball and the probability of drawing a black ball must equal 1.0 for both urns.

3.5   Methods for Estimating Subjective Probability Distributions

The methods which have been suggested in the literature for the assessment of subjective probability distributions can be divided into three categories:

   (i)   fixed interval methods;

   (ii) variable interval methods; and

   (iii) other methods.

Fixed Interval Methods

In fixed interval methods the range of all possible values of the variable is divided into a number of intervals (usually of equal width) and the assessor is asked to state, for each interval, his estimate of the probability that the value of the variable will lie in the interval. Suppose that the variable is market size, that the range of possible values is considered to be £17M – £22M, and that the following estimates are made:

Interval	Probability
£17M – £18M	0.1
£18M – £19M	0.4
£19M – £20M	0.2
£20M – £21M	0.2
£21M – £22M	0.1

The distribution shown in Fig. VI could be used for sampling.

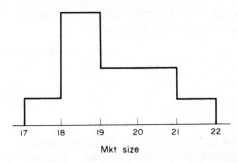

FIG. VI.   Probability distribution using fixed interval methods.

The order in which the intervals are presented to the assessor is thought to be an important consideration in fixed interval methods. Huber (1973) suggests that the assessor should first be asked to identify the least likely interval and to provide a probability for that interval. He should then be asked to identify the second least likely interval and to provide a probability for that interval, etc. This procedure, Huber says, may overcome the problem (to be discussed in more detail later in this chapter) that probability distributions with too small a variance are liable to be obtained if the assessor's attention is initially focused on central rather than extreme values of the distribution.

Variable Interval Methods

In variable interval methods the assessor is asked to identify intervals which correspond to given probabilities One of the ways of proceeding is described by Morrison (1967). First the assessor is asked for a value, say X, such that in his opinion the true value of the variable is just as likely to be above X as below X. (X is the median or 0.50 fractile of the distribution). The assessor is then told to ignore the possibility of the true value lying above X and asked to provide a value, say Y, which divides the range of values of the uncertain quantity below X into two equally likely parts (Y is the lower quartile or 0.25 fractile of the distribution). Similarly, he is asked to divide the range of all possible values above X into two equally likely parts in order to determine the 0.75 fractile. Other questions, if considered necessary, are then used to determine the 0.125, 0.375, 0.625 and 0.875 fractiles, etc.

In the example considered above, the following estimates might be made in the way which has just been described:

Fractile	Market Size
0.25	18.5
0.50	19.0
0.75	20.25

Assuming as before a range of 17M–22M, the cumulative probability distribution shown in Fig. VII could then be drawn.

Morrison's method (sometimes called the method of successive bisection) has the advantage that the assessor is only asked to think in terms

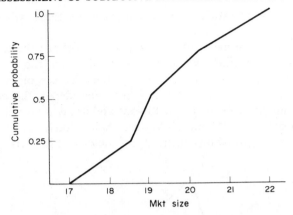

FIG. VII.   Cumulative distribution using variable interval methods.

of equally likely occurrences. Its disadvantage is that an error in one step of the procedure is carried forward to a later step. This has led to alternative variable interval methods being developed involving the use of questions such as:

"What value of the variable would you expect to be exceeded with a probability of 0.1."

However, such methods require judgements which are cognitively more difficult to make than the method of succession bisection.

Another disadvantage of Morrison's method has been found to be that it automatically focuses the assessor's initial attention on a central value of the distribution (i.e. the median) and thereby produces a distribution with too small a variance. In order to overcome this disadvantage Barclay and Peterson (1973) have suggested that the assessor should initially be asked to divide the range of possible values of the variable into three, rather than two, equally likely intervals. This produces a method known as the 'method of trisection'.

Other Methods

The fixed interval and variable interval method of assessment are the most widely used. A number of other methods have, however, been suggested in the literature and for completeness these will be briefly described.

In what might be termed "relative likelihood" methods, the assessor first estimates the most likely value of the variable (i.e. the mode of the distribution), and then estimates the relative chances of other values occurring. In the example which has been considered, the most likely market size might be estimated as £18.5M and it might also be estimated that market sizes of £18M and £20M were "half as likely" as £18.5M. This could lead to the probability distribution shown in Fig. VIII.

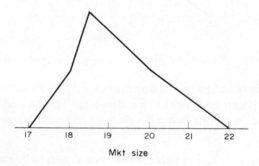

Mkt size

FIG. VIII.   Probability distribution using relative likelihood methods.

A method known as "psychometric ranking" was proposed by Smith (1967). In order to use the method, the assessor must first divide the range of all possible values of the variable into a number of intervals and then carry out a number of exercises aimed at ranking the intervals in order of ascending probability, and ranking the differences between the probabilities of adjacently ranked intervals in ascending order. Procedures are available for assigning probabilities to the intervals in a way which is consistent with the rankings.

Two further approaches known as the "equivalent prior sample" method and the "hypothetical future sample" method are occasionally suitable when the variable in question is a proportion. In the equivalent prior sample method the manager must make a statement of the form:

My uncertainty is equivalent to my having taken a sample of size n and having observed a proportion p.

For the hypothetical future sample method, the manager must answer a question of the form:

> How would your best estimate of the proportion change if I told you that, out of a sample of size n, a proportion p (different from your best estimate) had been observed.

Both methods use theory related to the Binomial distribution.

The "portrait method" of subjective probability assessment is described in Pouliquen (1970, p. 13). It involves asking the manager to choose, from a series of distributions which are displayed for him, a distribution of the right general shape.

Other methods of probability assessment which have been suggested involve betting or wagering. These are of limited interest as they nearly always require the analyst to make the somewhat doubtful assumption that the assessor wishes to maximise expected monetary value.

Finally, it is worth noting that some authors have looked for simpler approaches to assessing subjective probability distributions than those which have been suggested so far, because of the difficulties management experience when making detailed probability judgements. The use of the uniform distribution (see Fig. IX) based on an estimate of the range of the

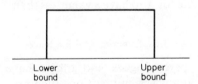

Lower   Upper
bound   bound

FIG. IX.   Uniform distribution

variable is suggested by Smith (1970). The use of a triangular distribution (see Fig. X) based on an estimate of the range of the variable and on an estimate of its most likely value is suggested by Smith (1970) and Eilon and Fowkes (1973). Allen (1968) has suggested the use of a trapezium-shaped distribution (see Fig. XI). He based this on the credibility and potential surprise concepts of Schackle (1961) and envisaged management using the following line of reasoning in arriving at Fig. XI.

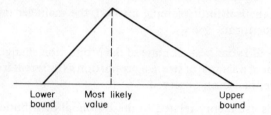

Lower   Most likely   Upper
bound   value   bound

FIG. X.   Triangular distribution

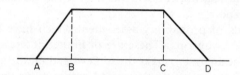

A   B   C   D

FIG. XI.   Allen's trapezium-shaped distribution

"On the basis of the information available to me at the present time, I consider any value of X between B and C to be completely credible (or alternatively I would not be at all surprised if the actual value of X turned out to be anywhere between B and C). I consider it to be utterly incredible for X to have a value less than A or greater than D."

3.6   Experimental Evidence

In recent years, psychologists and others have carried out many experiments aimed at answering questions such as:

(a) How good is man as an assessor of subjective probability distributions?

(b) Which of the available assessment procedures is the best?

(c) Can training improve man's performance at assessing subjective probability distributions?

The experiments have involved variables which are uncertain as far as the assessor is concerned, but which are such that the experimenter knows — or can find out — the true value.

One interesting feature of some of the experiments is the use of "scoring rules". These are functions of the true value of a variable and its assessed distribution which can be used both as a way of comparing the true value with the distribution and as a device for motivating the assessor. A discussion of scoring rules is contained in Savage (1971) and, more recently, Matheson and Winkler (1976). A scoring rule is "proper" if it is such that the assessor will maximise his subjectively expected score if, and only if, he reports his true opinions. Ideally, a scoring rule should be both proper and sensitive to the precise shape of the probability distribution which is assessed. Unfortunately, many of the scoring rules which have been suggested do not have the second of these two properties.

A complete survey of all the experiments which have been carried out would not be relevant to this book. (It is, in any case, questionable whether results obtained under "laboratory" conditions are relevant to the real world.) However, one result which crops up in nearly all of the experiments, and which cannot be ignored, is the tendency for individuals to assess distributions with too small a variance (i.e. distributions which are too narrow.) This phenomenon is known as "central bias" and will be discussed further in the next section.

Some experiments carried out in the 1960s by Alpert and Raiffa on Harvard graduate students, using variable interval methods, illustrate the "central bias" phenomenon well. Many different variables (e.g. the number of vehicles imported into US during 1967) were used. The results are summarised in Table 7. In the first group of assessments, only 33% (as opposed to the ideal 50%) assessed inter-quartile ranges which included the actual value, and 41% (as opposed to the ideal 2%) assessed distributions where the actual value fell outside the 0.01 and 0.99 fractiles. In the second group of assessments which took place after some training, these figures were improved to 43% and 23% respectively. One conclusion from the experiments is that the students were assessing 0.25 and 0.75 fractiles which were too tight (by fitting beta distributions to the fractiles assessed for proportions by a small sample of subjects, Alpert and Raiffa concluded that assessors tended to behave as though they knew approximately twice as much as they actually knew.) However, by far the most surprising conclusion to be drawn from the experiment is that the students were totally unable to assess the tails of the distributions. This inability was even more marked when the students were asked for 0.001 and 0.999 fractiles instead of 0.01 and 0.99 fractiles. Clearly, direct questions about tail probabilities are dangerous.

TABLE 7. RESULTS OF EXPERIMENTS BY ALPERT AND RAIFFA

	1st set of assessments (%)	2nd set of assessments (%)	Ideal (%)
Per cent of times value actually fell within interquartile range.	33	43	50
Per cent of times value actually fell outside range defined by 0.01 and 0.99 fractiles.	41	23	2

3.7 Biases

Conscious or subconscious discrepancies between an individual's expressed opinions and an accurate description of his underlying knowledge are known as biases. There are many different types of bias. Sometimes the whole distribution is shifted upwards or downwards relative to the "true" distribution. This is known as a displacement bias. On other occasions, the distribution is tighter (i.e. less spread out) than the true distribution. This is known as a central bias.

The sources of bias can be classified as motivational or cognitive. One example of motivational factors leading to a displacement bias was given in Section 3.2 when it was pointed out that, if an estimate is used as a basis for judging a manager's future performance, the manager is liable to be conservative (i.e. he is liable to make estimates which he knows he can beat). However, motivational factors can also lead to a central bias. For example, a manager may suppress the full range of his uncertainty because of a feeling that someone in his position should have a high degree of certainty about the variable under consideration.

Cognitive biases are caused by defects in the way in which a manager processes his perceptions about the variable under consideration. They can occur in a number of different ways. For example:

(a) An individual manager may allow himself to be unduly influenced by information which can easily be recalled or visualised. For instance, too much weight may be given to recent events and recent plans.

(b) The manager may form an initial basis for assessments and place too much emphasis on it. This is a particularly common bias and is known as "anchoring". It undoubtedly contributed significantly to the results of Alpert and Raiffa discussed in the previous section and to similar results obtained by other authors. It is now recognised that it is bad practice to focus the assessor's initial attention on a central value of the distribution, and the method of successive bisection (which was the method used by Alpert and Raiffa) is not now as popular as it used to be.

(c) The manager may be unable to distinguish adequately between distributions relating to the whole population and distributions relating to the average of the population. When monthly sales are being estimated, for example, there is a tendency to assess the same distribution for the average monthly sales during the year as for the sales in a particular month even though the former is far narrower.

(d) The manager may make unstated assumptions about the variable under consideration. For instance, judgements as to the market share of a new product may tacitly assume that no new competitors will enter the market.

(e) The manager may be unduly influenced by the way in which different scenarios of the future have been put to him.

Some good advice on how to overcome biases is offered by Spetzler and Stael von Holstein (1975). On the basis of their experience at the Stanford Research Institute these authors recommend that the interview between the analyst and the assessor should consist of five phases:

> motivating
> structuring
> conditioning
> encoding
> verifying.

During the motivating phase, the subject is introduced to the idea of probability assessment, and its importance in the investment decision under consideration is explained. Motivational biases are discussed openly and it is pointed out to the subject that a probability distribution does not entail a firm commitment on his part. The aim is simply to represent as clearly and as accurately as possible the complete judgement of the subject.

During the structuring stage the variable under consideration is clearly defined. This is very important. Spetzler and Stael von Holstein suggest that a good test to apply to any given definition is: could a clairvoyant reveal the value of the variable by specifying a single number and without requesting further clarification? A scale for measuring the variable which is familiar to the subject should also be chosen at this stage.

During the conditioning phase the analyst finds out what the subject is going to base his judgements on and cognitive biases are, wherever possible, nipped in the bud. One valuable procedure which the analyst can employ if the subject indicates that he is going to anchor on a particular value or place a great deal of emphasis on one particular aspect of the situation facing the company, is known as the use of availability. This involves asking the subject to construct scenarios corresponding to a number of different values — usually extreme values — for the variable.

As far as the encoding phase is concerned, Spetzler and Stael von Holstein recommend that both fixed interval and variable interval methods be used. To avoid anchoring they suggest that the extremes of the distribution should be established first:

> "Begin by asking the subject for what he considers to be extreme values for the uncertain quantity. Then ask for scenarios that might lead to outcomes outside those extremes. Also ask for the probabilities of outcomes outside the extremes. This deliberate use of availability is designed to counteract the central bias that is otherwise likely to occur. Eliciting the scenarios for extreme outcomes makes them available to the subject, and he is thus more likely to assign higher probabilities to extreme outcomes. This has the overall effect of increasing the variability of his assigned distribution for the variable."

Finally, in the verifying phase, tests are carried out to see whether the subject really believes the distribution. Some of these tests are likely to involve equally atttractive bets. If the subject proves to be uncomfortable with the final distribution it may be necessary to repeat some of the earlier phases.

3.8 Accuracy

There is little doubt that the biases discussed in the previous section are the main reasons why subjective probability distributions may not be an accurate reflection of managerial judgement. From the analytic point of view, however, it is worth noting that not all of the different procedures described in Section 3.5 are capable of assessing subjective probability distributions to the same accuracy.

Hull (1978) has investigated the way in which fifty-five beta distributions would be assessed using six different assessment procedures. He carried out two separate sets of analyses. The first assumed that the assessor was capable of making a finite number of infintely accurate probability assessments; the second assumed that the assessor made a finite number of assessments but that his ability to discriminate between different values of the variable and different probabilities was limited. In both cases, for the same number of assessments, fixed interval methods (with equal intervals being used) were found to provide better estimates of both the mean and the standard deviation of the distribution, than variable interval methods (with the method of successive bisection being used). Generally, it would seem that estimates of the mean and standard deviation are most accurate when the values of the variable at which cumulative probabilities are known are equally spaced. This conforms with intuition.

Table 8 summarises some of Hull's results. In addition to illustrating the points already mentioned, the table shows that it is more difficult to assess the mean of highly skewed distributions than it is to assess the mean of symmetrical or near-symmetrical distributions.

It will be noted from Table 8 that the average percentage error in the standard deviation is quite high — particularly for variable interval methods. If a piecewise quadratic (rather than a piecewise linear) cumulative distribution is fitted to assessments, the average error is much less (about 15% for fixed interval methods and about 20% for variable interval methods). The piecewise quadratic cumulative distribution is described in Schlaifer (1971, p. 225).

TABLE 8. AVERAGE ABSOLUTE ERRORS IN ESTIMATES OF MEAN AND
STANDARD DEVIATION WHEN FIVE PERFECTLY ACCURATE
ASSESSMENTS WERE MADE FOR FIFTY-FIVE DISTRIBUTIONS

	Highly skewed distributions		Symmetrical and nearly symmetrical distibutions	
	Error in mean (as per cent of range)	Per cent error in S.D.	Error in mean (as per cent of range)	Per cent error in S.D.
Fixed interval method (five assessments	0.2	24.5	0.0	23.2
Variable interval method (five assessments)	4.0	48.5	0.8	44.8

3.9   Optimistic and Pessimistic Estimates

We now consider the situation where a company is only interested in obtaining, say, 5% and 95% fractiles of a distribution in order to carry out a sensitivity analysis. Clearly many of the general points which have been made in connection with the assessment of complete distributions still apply. It is important to define the variable clearly and unambiguously. Motivational and cognitive biases should be identified and where possible eliminated. To avoid "anchoring", the assessor's attention should initially be directed towards extreme values. This means that ideally the 5% and 95% fractiles should be obtained *before* the most likely values are considered.

It is essential that the analyst first allow the assessor to appreciate the full range of his uncertainty. How bad could the variable get? Under what circumstances do you think that might happen? Could the value in fact turn out to be even worse? These are useful opening questions when a pessimistic estimate is being elicited. Of course the most difficult task for the analyst at this stage is to get the assessor to think of a few extreme scenarios without actually leading him.

The next stage is to home in on a number which will form the pessimistic estimate. The assessor must appreciate that there should only be a 5% or 1 in 20 chance of the actual value of the variable being worse than the pessimistic estimate. If the assessor is a gambler then betting odds might be useful here. It should be noted that 1 in 20 is a much smaller probability than many people realise. The chance of two dice showing a 6 and a 5, for example, is at 1 in 18 better than 1 in 20.

A similar procedure is followed as far as the optimistic estimate is concerned and, finally, the assessor is encouraged to give his "best guess" or "most likely value" for the variable. As a final test the analyst can ask the assessor whether he would rather bet on the value of the variable being greater than his pessimistic, or less than his optimistic estimate. This often results in the pessimistic estimate being revised.

3.10 Summary

The realism of an investment appraisal depends to a large extent on the accuracy of the estimates which are made for the variables. Although occasionally estimates can be based on analysis of past data, analysts must usually rely heavily on judgements made by managers. Whether the judgements are providing optimistic and pessimistic estimates for a sensitivity analysis, or complete probability distributions for a risk simulation, the way in which the judgements are obtained is crucially important. The analyst should always be aware of possible motivational and cognitive biases and take steps to minimise or eliminate them.

If a complete subjective probability distribution is required, the analyst has the choice between using fixed interval and variable interval methods of assessment. Fixed interval methods have the advantage that they are inherently more accurate and do not focus on central values of the distribution initially. Variable interval methods have the advantage that the assessor need only think in terms of equally likely events.

References

ALLEN, D. H. (1968). Credibility forecasts and their application to the economic assessment of novel reseach and development projects, *Operational Research Quarterly*, vol. 19, no. 1, pp. 25–42.

ALPERT, M. and RAIFFA, H. (1969). *A progress report on the training of probability assessors*, unpublished paper, Harvard Business School.

BARCLAY, S. and PETERSON, C. R. (1973). *Two methods for assessing probability distributions*, Decisions and Designs Inc. Technical Report 73–1, Aug.

BASS, F. M. (1969). A new product growth model for consumer durables, *Management Science*, vol. 15, no. 5, pp. 215–27.

BROWN, B. and HELMAR, O. (1962). *Improving the reliability of estimates obtained from a consensus of experts*, Rand California.

CHAMBERS, J. C., MULLICK, S. K. and SMITH, D. D. (1971). How to choose the right forecasting technique, *Harvard Business Review*, July–Aug.

DALKEY, N. and HELMAR, O. (1963). An experimental application of the Delphi methods to the use of experts, *Management Science*, vol. 9, pp. 458–67.

EILON, S. and FOWKES, T. R. (1973). Sampling procedures for risk simulations, *Operational Research Quarterly*, vol. 24, no. 2, pp. 241–52.

HUBER, G. P. (1974). Methods for quantifying probabilities and multivariate utilities, *Decision Sciences*, vol. 5, pp. 430–58.

HULL, J. C. (1978). The accuracy of the means and standard deviations of subjective probability distributions, *Journal of the Royal Statistical Society*, A, vol. 141, no. 1, pp. 79–85.

HUSSEY, D. E. (1974). *Corporate planning: Theory and Practice*, Pergamon Press, Oxford.

MATHESON, J. E. and WINKLER, R. L. (1976). Scoring rules for continuous probability distributions, *Management Science*, vol. 22, B, no. 10, pp. 1087–96.

MOORE, P. G. and THOMAS, H. (1975). Measuring uncertainty, *OMEGA*, vol. 3, no. 6, pp. 657–72.

MORRISON, D. G. (1967). Critique of ranking procedures and subjective probability distributions, *Management Science*, vol. 14, B, no. 4, pp. 253–4.

POULIQUEN, L. Y. (1970). *Risk analysis in project appraisal*, Johns Hopkins Press for the International Bank for Reconstruction and Development.

SAVAGE, L. J. (1971). Evaluation of personal probabilities and expectations, *Journal of American Statistical Association*, vol. 66, pp. 783–801.

SCHACKLE, G. L. S. (1961). *Decision order and time in human affairs*, Cambridge University Press.

SCHAIFER, R. (1971). *Computer programs for elementary decision analysis*, Division of Research Harvard.

SMITH, L. E. (1967). Ranking procedures and subjective probability distributions, *Management Science*, B, vol. 14, no. 4, pp. 236–49.

SMITH, M. B. (1970). Probability models for petroleum investment decisions, *Journal of Petroleum Technology*, May, pp. 545–550.

SPETZLER, C. S. and STAEL VON HOLSTEIN, C. S. (1975). Probability encoding in decision analysis, *Management Science*, vol. 22, no. 3, pp. 340–58.

WOODS, D. H. (1966). Improving estimates that involve uncertainty, *Harvard Business Review*, July–Aug., pp. 91–8.

Chapter 4
DEALING WITH DEPENDENCE IN
RISK SIMULATION

4.1 Introduction

Two variables in an investment project are dependent if a knowledge of the value of one of them would influence estimates made for the other. To make this more explicit, suppose that two variables in a certain investment situation are "life of plant" and "residual value of plant". Our best estimate for the life of the plant might be 20 years and our best estimate for its residual value might be £20,000. A question which arises is: "What would happen if we were told tomorrow that the life of the plant will in fact be 15 years?" If this would cause us to change our best estimate of the residual value then the two variables are dependent. On the other hand, if our estimate for the residual value would remain the same regardless of the life of the plant, the two variables are independent.

Dependencies cause problems in risk simulation because, when they are present, it is not correct to sample independently from the probability distributions of the different variables. Suppose that, in the example which has just been given, "residual value of plant" is found to be dependent on "life of plant". Theoretically, the simulation should first sample from the distribution for the life of the plant and then, depending on the precise value obtained, choose an appropriate distribution for residual value and sample from it.

This chapter is concerned with practical approaches for dealing with dependencies in risk simulation. It starts by considering the extent to which dependencies are liable to affect the distribution of NPV. It then discusses various ways of avoiding complex sampling schemes involving conditional probability distributions. Finally, it reviews critically some of the sampling schemes which have been suggested in the literature. One particular sampling scheme which the author has on occasion used successfully is described in Appendix C.

4.2   The Importance of Dependencies

To provide an indication of the potential importance of dependencies in a risk evaluation study, Hull (1976) has investigated the effect of assuming total positive dependence between each pair of variables in the famous case study described in Hertz (1964). (The precise meaning of the term "total positive dependence" will be given in the next section.) The Hertz case study concerns a proposed $10 million extension to a chemical processing plant. There are nine uncertain variables: the initial market size ('000s tons), the market growth (% p.a.), the selling price ($ per ton), the market share (%), the initial investment ($M), the life of investment (yrs.), residual value ($M), operating costs ($ per ton), and fixed costs ($'000s p.a.).

The results obtained are summarised in Tables 9 and 10. Triangular distributions were used for the variables with 1000 simulation runs being

TABLE 9. INCREASE IN MEAN OF NPV IN HERTZ MODEL IF TOTAL POSITIVE DEPENDENCE BETWEEN TWO VARIABLES ($M)

	Initial market size	Market growth	Selling price	Market share	Initial investment	Life of investment	Residual value	Operating costs	Fixed costs
Initial market size		0	1.6	0.7	0	0.2	0	−1.4	0
Market growth			1.0	0.6	0	0.2	0	−1.0	0
Selling price				1.9	0	0.9	0	0	0
Market share					0	0.2	0	−1.2	0
Initial investment						0	0	−0.2	0
Life of investment							0	−1.6	0
Residual value								−0.1	0
Operating costs									0
Fixed costs									

TABLE 10. INCREASE IN STANDARD DEVIATION OF NPV IN HERTZ
MODEL IF TOTAL POSITIVE DEPENDENCE BETWEEN TWO
VARIABLES ($M)

	Initial market size	Market growth	Selling price	Market share	Initial investment	Life of investment	Residual value	Operating costs	Fixed costs
Initial market size		0.2	1.5	1.4	-0.1	0.4	0	-0.4	0
Market growth			1.0	0.9	0	0.2	0	0.4	0
Selling price				1.4	-0.5	0.2	0.1	-6.8	-0.1
Market share					-0.1	0.4	0	0	0
Initial investment						0	0	0.9	0
Life of investment							0	0.7	0
Residual value								0.2	0
Operating costs									0.1
Fixed costs									

carried out. With no dependencies the distribution of NPV has, in $M, a mean of -2.7 and a standard deviation of 9.5.

Two points emerge from Tables 9 and 10.

(i) The effect of a dependence between two variables can be very great indeed. Consider the two variables "selling price" and "operating costs". Total positive dependence between them would reduce the standard deviation of NPV by about 72%.

(ii) Many of the potential dependencies in the Hertz model are not very important. If we arbitrarily define a dependence as insignificant when its effect on both the mean and standard deviation of NPV is less than $0.25M, then it can be seen that the majority of the potential dependencies in the Hertz model (21 out of 36) are insignificant.

It is necessary for the analyst to distinguish important dependencies from unimportant ones at an early stage so that management are not asked to provide a large number of assessments which are irrelevant to the decision under consideration.

4.3 Evaluating the Importance of a Dependence

It would be particularly convenient if the output from a sensitivity analysis could be used to predict the importance of a particular dependence. Chapter 5 discusses *inter alia* the extent to which this is possible. It concludes that a sensitivity analysis can, in many cases, be used to provide a rough indication of the effect of a dependence on the standard deviation of NPV. But it cannot be used to indicate the effect of the dependence on the mean of NPV or on any other characteristic of the distribution of NPV.

Generally, it would seem unlikely that a dependence between two variables which are revealed to be relatively unimportant by a sensitivity analysis will itself be important. If the analyst has doubts about the importance of a particular dependence, one useful idea involves assessing independent distributions for all the variables in the usual way and then comparing:

(a) the distribution of NPV obtained assuming no dependence; and

(b) the distribution of NPV obtained assuming total dependence.

If there is very little difference between (a) and (b), then the effect of the dependence can be ignored and no managerial time need be wasted in quantifying the "extent of the dependence" accurately. If (a) and (b) are markedly different, then this is an indication that some effort should be expended in modelling the dependence.

The approach which has just been described can be particularly useful if there is only one dependence of any importance. If, for that dependence, both (a) and (b) lead to the same decision (accept or reject) on the investment, then no further work need be carried out. This illustrates the important general principle that extra assessments by management and further work by the analyst are only of value when they have some chance of changing the decision taken; a perfectly accurate distribution of the performance measure is not of value in itself.

Total dependence between two variables X and Y (see (b) above) needs careful defining. It is not useful to define it as the situation where ρ, the coefficient of correlation, equals either +1 or –1 as this implies that:

$$Y = a + b X \qquad\qquad a,\ b \text{ constant } b \neq 0$$

and means that the independent distributions of X and Y must be of the same shape. A more useful definition would seem to be as follows:

> X and Y are totally positively dependent if, when X takes a value equal to its kth fractile, Y also takes a value equal to its kth fractile. X and Y are totally negatively dependent if when X takes a value equal to its kth fractile, Y takes a value equal to its $(1-k)$th fractile.

This allows two distributions of quite different shapes to be "perfectly dependent". When the independent distributions of X and Y happen to be of the same shape then total dependence, as has just been defined, implies that ρ equals +1 or –1.

4.4   The Level of Disaggregation

In this section and the next we consider two factors which are, in part, under the control of the analyst and which influence critically the total number of dependencies in a risk simulation.

By "level of disaggregation" in a cash flow model we mean the degree of detail in that model. Generally speaking, the more disaggregated a model is, the more variables it includes. The model constructed by Hertz (1964) has by most standards a fairly low level of disaggregation. It would be more disaggregated if the market were split up in some way with several different initial market sizes, several market growth rates and several different market shares being included as variables in the model. It would also be more disaggregated if several different categories of costs were considered with, say, labour costs and material costs being distinguished from other operating costs.

What is the right level of disaggregation? This is a crucial question. It is generally true that the more disaggregated a model is, the easier it is for managers to make accurate judgements about the probability distributions of different variables. But it is also true that an increase in disaggregation tends to lead to an increase in the number of dependencies. Suppose that the Hertz model were disaggregated by considering separately market A and market B. Although management might find it easier to make estimates for variables, many "messy" dependencies would almost certainly have to be considered. The initial size of market A might be dependent on that of market B; the growth rate of market A might be dependent on that of market B; the company's share of market A might be dependent on its share of market B; the prices in markets A and B might be dependent, etc.

The choice of a level of disaggregation requires a trade-off between the advantages of clarity of managerial judgement and the advantages of having relatively few dependencies. In view of the complications which dependencies give rise to, it seems sensible to limit disaggregation as far as is possible without asking managers to make judgements about unfamiliar variables. Of course, if disaggregation is limited too much the essential advantage of the risk simulation approach will be lost. The ultimate in a non-disaggregated model would be one where managers have to make judgements about NPV directly. This would certainly avoid all dependencies — but it is of questionable value.

4.5 Isolating Sources of Uncertainty

The way in which the analyst chooses the variables in the cash flow model can have a considerable influence on the number of dependencies. Ideally, the variables which are defined should represent different independent sources of uncertainty. (The purpose of risk simulation is to disaggregate uncertainty — not to disaggregate a project into its technological components.)

One example of how a source of uncertainty might be identified is provided by the Hertz model. Suppose that operating costs and price are considered to be interdependent. It is likely that the true source of the uncertainty would be identified by defining a new variable X as follows:

X = Price per ton — operating costs per ton

or possibly as:

$$X = \frac{\text{Price per ton}}{\text{Operating costs per ton}}$$

(Note that the Hertz model assumes price to be an uncontrollable variable; very often it will be a decision variable.)

Another example is provided by the Port of Mogadiscio study described in Pouliquen (1970). In the study there was uncertainty as to the number of men which would be required in the port in gangs, in transit sheds, in warehouses, etc. Instead of defining "men in transit sheds", "men in warehouses", etc., as separate variables and then trying to quantify dependences between them, the analyst recognised that the real sources of uncertainty were:

(a)   the number of men required in gangs, in transit sheds in warehouses, etc., assuming efficient operation; and

(b)   the Port Authority's efficiency at eliminating redundant labour.

Variables were defined accordingly and problems arising from dependencies between variables were eliminated.

There seems little doubt that the isolation of independent sources of uncertainty, if it is feasible, is by far the most satisfactory way of dealing with dependence.

4.6 Sampling Schemes Suggested In The Literature

A number of methods, none of them wholly satisfactory, have been suggested for constructing a sampling scheme to deal with partial dependence between two variables.

Hertz (1964) suggests that a single subjective probability distribution be assessed for the independent variable and that several conditional subjective probability distributions be assessed for the dependent variable, each of these being conditional on the independent variable lying within a different interval. On each run of the simulation the value sampled for the independent variable would then determine the particular conditional subjective probability distribution used. The major drawback of this procedure is that it involves management in making an unreasonably large number of individual probability assessments.

Eilon and Fowkes (1973) consider the problem of dependence in some detail and suggest a number of different discriminant sampling procedures where the range of possible values of the dependent variable is restricted in some way according to the value sampled for the independent variable. This is a sensible idea. It has the disadvantage that a particular discriminant sampling scheme cannot easily be related to a judgement by management as to "the extent of the dependence". Also, if the unconditional distribution of the dependent variable has been assessed in advance it is sometimes difficult to choose the scheme so as to satisfy the consistency condition:

$$g\ (V_2) = \int_{-\infty}^{+\infty} h\ (V_2/V_1)\, f\ (V_1)\, d\, V_1 \qquad (4.1)$$

where g is the unconditional distribution of the dependent variable (V_2), f is the distribution of the independent variable (V_1) and h is the conditional distribution of V_2 given the value of V_1.

Kryzanowski et al. (1972) suggest the following procedure when the value of the independent variable is less than its 0.50 fractile:

(i) if the intensity of the dependence is "slight", sample in such a way that the probability of the dependent variable being less than its 0.50 fractile is 0.60 for positive dependence and 0.40 for negative dependence.

(ii) if the intensity of the dependence is "moderate", sample in such a way that the probability of the dependent variable being less than its 0.50 fractile is 0.75 for positive dependence and 0.25 for negative dependence.

(iii) if the intensity of the dependence is "high", sample in such a way that the probability of the dependent variable being less than its 0.50 fractile is 0.90 for positive dependence and 0.10 for negative dependence.

Similar rules are suggested when the independent variable is greater than its 0.50 fractile. The procedures satisfy the condition in Equation (4.1). Their main disadvantage would seem to be that the terms "slight", "moderate" and "high" are imprecise.

Finally, it is worth noting that, if data are available on two dependent variables, it can be analysed and used to construct a sampling scheme. Unfortunately situations where past data, without any managerial judgement, can be used as a predictor of the future are all too few.

4.7   Proposal for a Sampling Scheme

Suppose that variable V_2 is considered to depend on variable V_1 in a risk simulation and that unconditional distributions for V_1 and V_2 have already been assessed by management. One of the simplest single assessments of the extent of the dependence of V_2 on V_1 which can be made by management is the following:

$$\text{``assuming } V_1 = Q \text{ my median estimate for } V_2 \text{ is } P\text{''} \qquad (4.2)$$

where Q is a value in one of the tails of the distribution of V_1.

Appendix C shows that if an assessment such as that in Equation (4.2) is made, then it is possible to find a set of conditional distributions for V_2 which are both consistent with the assessment and with the unconditional distributions of V_2 and V_1. This gives rise to a new sampling scheme which overcomes some of the drawbacks of the schemes mentioned in the previous section because:

(a) it takes account of a numerical estimate of the extent of the dependence;

(b) it gives rise to conditional distributions which satisfy the consistency condition in Equation (4.1).

A fuller discussion of this idea is given in Hull (1977).

4.8   The Growth-Rate Problem

A related problem to that of dealing with dependences in risk evaluation is what might be termed "the growth-rate problem". This will now be described and discussed.

In risk evaluation the value of a variable such as "sales" or "unit cost" in any one year is often considered to depend on its value in one or more previous years. It is customary to take account of this by describing the variable in terms of a distribution of its initial value and a distribution of its percentage annual growth rate. There are, however, several difficulties as far as this practice is concerned. For a start, the meaning of the term "the distribution of the percentage annual growth rate" may be unclear to the assessor. Indeed, different writers on risk analysis have used the term in different ways. Wagle (1967) in an analysis of the Hertz model assumes that the distribution of the market growth rate in any one year is independent of that in any other year. Other authors who have analysed the same model using risk simulation assume that the market growth rate is constant over the life of the project (i.e. that it is only necessary to sample from the distribution once during each simulation run).

If it is decided that this latter interpretation of the distribution of the percentage annual growth rate is appropriate, then it must be recognised that the growth rate will not, in practice, be exactly constant over the life of the project and that any assessments which management make will correspond to an "average" growth rate. The question then arises as to whether there are biases in the way managers assess average growth rates from the scenarios of the future which they have in their minds. In this connection it is worth noting that, because of discounting, departures from the average growth curve early in a project's life are likely to be more important than departures later in the project's life.

Another problem with the models which are usually assumed is that management may not expect the average growth rate to remain constant over time. The new product life-cycle phenomena has already been discussed in Section 3.2 and it seems likely that very often if a variable such as "sales" or "market size" is involved a pattern such as that in Figure V, will be anticipated.

One possible solution to this problem is to identify the growth parameters and ask management to provide distributions for them. With a new product the relevant parameters might be "the initial growth rate" and "the maximum sales". Alternatively, the following model suggested by Bass (1969) might be usable:

$$S(T) = [m(p + q)^2/p] \; e^{-(p+q)^T} \; (q/p \; e^{-(p+q)^T} + 1)^2$$

where $S(T)$ is the total sales at time T and m, p and q are constants. p is the "coefficient of innovation", q is the "coefficient of imitation" and m is related to the peak sales.

Another approach to the non-constant growth-rate problem is to divide the total life of the project into several parts and to obtain a probability distribution for the growth rate corresponding to each part. However, this does have drawbacks as the growth rate during one part of the project's life will clearly depend on that during other parts.

Another possibility is to define a family of non-exponential growth curves (see Figure XII) for the variable under consideration. The "median" growth curve, the "upper quartile" growth curve and the "lower quartile" growth curve could be assessed using a similar approach to that for assessing the 0.5, 0.75, 0.25 fractiles of an ordinary distribution. Packages such as ICL's PROSPER tend to encourage the use of families of growth curves.

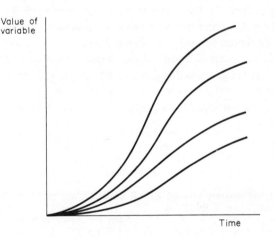

Fig. XII.   A family of growth curves.

Yet another alternative to the use of the "initial value" + "constant growth rate" model is the use of a model of probabilistic growth. A number of different models of probabilistic growth have been described in articles concerned with capacity expansion such as Manne (1961) and Giglio

(1970). A further one can be based on the model of dependence presented in Appendix C and is briefly described at the end of that Appendix.

4.9   Summary

Whenever possible a detailed modelling of the dependence between two variables should be avoided. Potential dependencies should always be considered when the risk evaluation model is first formulated. Disaggregation should be limited as far as is reasonable and the analyst should attempt to define variables which correspond to the individual sources of uncertainty.

Once a dependence between two variables has been identified in a model the first step should be to determine whether it is likely to be important. If a sensitivity analysis indicates that the two variables are relatively unimportant as far as the total project risk is concerned, then it is unlikely that the dependence is worth worrying about. However, if the analyst has any doubts on this score he can compare the results of simulations which assume no dependence and total dependence.

When it is necessary to model dependence, a number of approaches are possible. These range from discriminant sampling schemes where the value of the dependent variable is restricted in some way according to the value sampled for the independent variable to a model such as that outlined in Appendix C.

References

BASS, F. M. (1969). A new product growth model for consumer durables, *Management Science,* vol. 15, no. 5, pp. 215–27

EILON, S. and FOWKES, T. R. (1973). Sampling procedures for risk simulation, *Operational Research Quarterly,* vol. 24, no. 2, pp. 241–52.

GIGLIO, R. J. (1970). Stochastic Capacity Models, *Management Science,* vol. 17, no. 3, pp. 174–84.

HERTZ, D. B. (1964). Risk analysis in capital investment, *Harvard Business Review,* Jan.–Feb., pp. 95–106.

HULL, J. C. (1976). *A study of the subjective probability assessments necessary for the analysis of the risk in major capital investment opportunities,* PhD Thesis, Cranfield Institute of Technology.

HULL, J. C. (1977). Dealing with dependence in risk simulation, *Operational Research Quarterly,* vol. 28, 1ii, pp. 201–13.

KRYZANOWSKI, L., LUSZTIG, P. and SCHWAB, B. (1972). Monte Carlo simulation and capital investment decisions — a case study, *Engineeering Economist*, vol. 18, no. 1, pp. 31–47.

MANNE, A. S. (1961). Capacity expansion and probabilistic growth, *Econometrica*, vol. 29, no. 4, pp. 632–49.

POULIQUEN (1970). *Risk analysis in project appraisal*, Johns Hopkins Press for the International Bank for Reconstruction and Development.

WAGLE, B. (1967). A statistical analysis of risk in capital investment projects, *Operational Research Quarterly*, vol. 18, no. 1, pp. 13–33.

Chapter 5
USING THE RESULTS FROM A SENSITIVITY ANALYSIS

5.1. Introduction

A sensitivity analysis is usually one of the first steps in an evaluation of the risk in a capital investment opportunity. This chapter describes some research carried out by the author into the question of how the output from a sensitivity analysis should be interpreted and used. As we shall see, the research indicates that a sensitivity analysis can considerably simplify the risk evaluation process. Indeed, it is often true that once a sensitivity analysis has been carried out, sufficient information is obtained to render any further analysis of the risk in the investment unnecessary.

Three questions are to be considered in this chapter:

(i) To what extent can a sensitivity analysis be used to provide a rough measure of the total uncertainty in the performance measure?

(ii) To what extent does the output from a sensitivity analysis provide a good indication of the effects of errors in the distributions of different variables on the distribution of the performance measure?

(iii) To what extent does the output from a sensitivity analysis provide good indications as to the effect of dependences between different variables on the distribution of the performance measure?

First, some results are produced for the simple situation where the performance measure depends linearly on the variables, and then the extent to which the results can be extended to apply to other more complicated situations is tested empirically using four case studies.

The material in this chapter is also presented in Hull (1978).

5.2. Carrying out the Sensitivity Analysis

The way in which a sensitivity analysis should be carried out has already been discussed in some detail in Chapter 2. However, it will be useful at this stage to repeat some of the main arguments algebraically.

Suppose that P is the performance measure, that $X_1, X_2 \ldots X_m$ are the uncertain variables and that:

$$P = f(X_1, X_2 \ldots X_m)$$

A sensitivity analysis generally calculates for each variable j:

$$f(E_1, E_2 \ldots E_{j-1}, E_j + \Delta E_j, E_{j+1} \ldots E_m) - f(E_1, E_2 \ldots E_m)$$

where E_j is the most likely estimate of X_j and ΔE_j is a change in the value of E_j.

The question of how the magnitudes of the ΔE_js should be chosen was discussed in Section 2.2. It was concluded that choosing ΔE_j as a fixed percentage of E_j for all j is not the best way of proceeding as it does not relate the errors considered to the uncertainties which management attach to their estimates of individual variables. Ideally, management should make in addition to a best estimate, E_j, pessimistic and optimistic estimates L_j and U_j for each variable j. Measures S_j ($j = 1 \ldots m$) can then be defined as follows:

$$S_j = f(E_1, E_2 \ldots E_{j-1}, U_j, E_{j+1} \ldots E_m) - f(E_1, E_2 \ldots E_{j-1}, L_j, E_{j+1} \ldots E_m)$$

and can be used to provide an indication of the relative importance of different variables.

To ease exposition, U_j is defined equal to the higher of the optimistic and pessimistic estimates, and L_j is equal to the lower of the two. (The optimistic estimate for a variable is not always higher than its pessimistic estimate; for variables such as costs the reverse is true).

The difference between U_j and L_j will be referred to as the range of variable j. S_j will be referred to as its sensitivity coefficient.

5.3. Results for a Simple Linear Model

In this section we consider the model:

$$P = f(X_1, X_2 \ldots X_m) = \sum_{j=1}^{m} a_j X_j$$

where the a_js are constant and the X_js are independent. This model is only appropriate in relatively simple situations (e.g. those where P is net present value and each X_j represents an inflow or outflow of cash occurring in one or more years). However, it is worth examining the model in detail because it suggests results which might be approximately true in a wide range of situations.

It is easy to see that the model implies:

$$S_j = a_j (U_j - L_j) \tag{5.1}$$

Furthermore:

$$\mu_p = \sum_{j=1}^{m} a_j \mu_j \tag{5.2}$$

$$\sigma_p^2 = \sum_{j=1}^{m} a_j^2 \sigma_j^2 \tag{5.3}$$

where μ_p and σ_p are the mean and standard deviation of P and μ_j and σ_j are the mean and standard deviation of X_j. Defining:

$$k_j = \frac{\sigma_j}{U_j - L_j}$$

for all j it follows from equations (5.1) and (5.3) that

$$\sigma_p^2 = \sum_{j=1}^{m} k_j^2 S_j^2 \tag{5.4}$$

This is an interesting result as it shows that an estimate of σ_p can be obtained from the sensitivity coefficients and estimates of the k_js. If we assume that k_j is approximately constant for all j (i.e. that a standard deviation of a variable is approximately proportional to its range) then Equation (5.4) implies that it is the square of the sensitivity coefficient of variable j which in effect determines the contribution of variable j to σ_p^2. If one variable has half the sensitivity coefficient of another variable then its contribution to σ_p^2 will be one-quarter as much, etc. This is encouraging. It means that, for the linear model, the less sensitive variables contribute very little to the overall uncertainty.

A number of other results can be obtained by straightforward analysis. Suppose

p_j is the error in μ_j expressed as a fraction of the range of X_j, and

q_j is the error in σ_j expressed as a fraction of σ_j,

it can be shown that:

   (i) the effect of error p_j on μ_p is equal to $p_j S_j$;

   (ii) the effect of error p_j on σ_p is zero;

   (iii) the effect of error q_j on μ_p is zero;

   (iv) the effect of error q_j on σ_p is approximately equal to

$$\frac{q_j \, k_j^2 \, S_j^2}{\sigma_p}.$$

Again, we see that in matters connected with σ_p it is S_j^2 and not S_j which is important. Suppose as before that one variable has half the sensitivity coefficient of another variable. The result in (iv) above shows that a certain percentage error in the standard deviation of the first variable will have approximately one-quarter the effect on σ_p as the same percentage error for the second variable.

Suppose next that X_j and X_k are dependent with coefficient of correlation ρ_{jk}. It can be shown that:

   (i) the effect of this dependence on μ_p is zero;

   (ii) the effect of this dependence on σ_p is approximately

$$\frac{S_j \, S_k \, k_j \, k_k \, \rho_{jk}}{\sigma_p}.$$

This is also an interesting result. It implies that (if k_j is approximately constant for all j) the effect of a dependence between variables j and k on the standard deviation of the performance measure is approximately proportional to the product of the coefficient of correlation and $S_j S_k$.

5.4 Case Studies Investigated

A number of powerful results have now been produced for the linear model and it is clearly worth investigating the extent to which they hold true in the situations which are actually encountered in practice. Four risk evaluation case studies (to be referred to as cases A–D) will therefore be examined in detail

Case A is the case study in Hertz (1964). This has already been described in Section 4.2. A total of nine uncertain variables are involved.

Case B is a well-documented case study described in Kryzanowski *et al.* (1972). A major natural resource firm is considering proposals for expanding its plant, and detailed probability assessments are made for twelve uncertain variables: price, price growth rate, variable operating costs at present, three different categories of additional variable operating costs, extra fixed costs, cost growth rate, capital costs, production, life of project and additional working capital.

Case C is based on Vandell (1970). It concerns a proposed investment in an advertising campaign for a consumer product. There are seven uncertain variables: initial market size, market growth, market share, price adjustment factor, cost of goods sold, variable selling expenses and fixed costs. One feature of this investment is that if sales are not up to expectations, it can be abandoned at very little cost.

Case D is based on Economos (1968). A large corporation has to decide whether to acquire a computer leasing subsidiary. The subsidiary would satisfy the computing needs of the corporation as well as competing in external markets. There are four uncertain variables: the rate of growth of the total US computer industry, the rate of growth of the corporation's computer requirements, the year of the "hostile act" (computer manufacturers' act to impede the growth of leasing companies) and the year of the introduction of fourth generation equipment.

All the case studies involve cash flow models which are non-linear. It is interesting to note that in case D the model is what might be termed "highly non-linear" with each of the variables being either a growth rate or a year in which an event happens.

5.5. Approximating to the Standard Deviation of the Performance Measure

The first key result produced in Section 5.3 for the linear model was:

$$\sigma_p = \sqrt{\sum_{j=1}^{m} k_j^2 S_j^2} \tag{5.5}$$

In this section we explore whether this formula would provide an approximate guide as to the value of σ_p in the case studies described in the previous section.

The estimates assumed for the variables in the case studies are shown in Tables 11 to 14. These tables also show the values of the sensitivity coefficients calculated for the variables. In cases A and D two performance measures were considered: NPV with a discount rate of 10% and IRR. In cases B and C only NPV with a discount rate of 10% was considered. (This was because, in cases B and C, there was a significant probability that all the cash flows would have the same sign and that a finite real value of IRR would not, in consequence, exist.

TABLE 11. DATA FOR CASE A

Variable, j	U_j	E_j	L_j	Sens. coeff. S_j if: NPV (10% disc rate)	IRR
Initial market size ('000 tons)	340	250	100	14,870	27.3
Market growth (% p.a.)	6	3	0	3587	5.2
Selling price ($ per ton)	575	510	385	39,237	92.2
Market share (%)	17	12	3	18,070	34.1
Initial investment ($M)	10.5	9.5	7.0	3500	11.2
Life of investment (yrs)	15	10	5	8287	8.9
Residual value ($M)	5.0	4.5	3.5	578	0.6
Operating costs ($ per ton)	545	435	370	36,139	79.4
Fixed costs ($'000s p.a.)	375	300	250	768	1.4

TABLE 12. DATA FOR CASE B

Variable, j	U_j	E_j	L_j	Sens. coeff. S_j if: NPV (10% disc rate)
Price of product ($ per unit)	140	128	115	5418
Price growth rate (% p.a.)	4.6	2.7	0	12,412
Variable operating cost now ($ per unit)	55	51	48	1502
Extra variable operating costs 1 (% per unit)	10.0	6.25	3.75	1341
Extra variable operating costs 2 ($ per unit)	37.5	25.0	22.5	3218
Extra variable operating costs 3 ($ per unit)	2.5	0.38	0	536
Extra fixed costs ($'000s p.a.)	320	170	120	1913
Cost growth rate (% p.a.)	8.3	2.6	-0.3	20,449
Capital costs in year 0 ($'000s)	1165	965	565	1479
Production in year 1 (units)	27,000	15,000	5000	14,684
Life of project (yrs)	40	30	15	3247
Extra working capital in year 0 ($'000s)	173	123	43	356

TABLE 13. DATA FOR CASE C

Variable, j	U_j	E_j	L_j	Sens. coeff. S_j if: NPV (10% disc rate)
Initial market size (lire M)	12,000	10,000	8000	186.4
Market growth (% p.a.)	9	3	-3	119.0
Market share (%)	7	5	3	319.8
Price adjustment factor (%)	5	1	-5	41.9
Cost of goods sold (% of sales)	58	56	54	102.4
Variable selling expenses (% of sales)	19	17	15	102.4
Fixed costs (lire M. p.a.)	35	28	21	85.8

TABLE 14. DATA FOR CASE D

Variable, j	U_j	E_j	L_j	Sens. coeff. S_j if: NPV (disc rate = 10%)	IRR
Rate of growth of external market (% p.a.)	10	5	3	1386	0.9
Rate of growth of internal market (% p.a.)	10	5	3	867	0.6
Year of hostile act	4	2	1	3813	2.2
Year of introduction of fourth generation equipment	6	3	1	6328	4.7

The variables in the case studies were, for the purposes of this exercise, assumed to have independent triangular distributions and 2000 Monte Carlo simulation runs were carried out to calculate distributions for the performance measures.

Tables 15 and 16 compare the values of σ_p calculated using Equations (5.5) with the simulated values. The latter have a standard error of approximately 0.022 σ_p and can be assumed to all intents and purposes to be "correct". Exact values for the k_js were calculated from known properties of the triangular distribution for the purpose of using Equation (5.5).

Tables 15 and 16 show that Equation (5.5), assuming accurate k_j s are available, can be used to provide a rough indication as to the standard deviation of both NPV and IRR in the case studies. As might be expected, the percentage errors in the estimates which are made on average higher for IRR than for NPV.

TABLE 15. ACCURACY OF APPROXIMATE
APPROACH TO ESTIMATING THE
STANDARD DEVIATION OF NPV
(DISC RATE = 10%)

| Case study | Standard deviation of NPV calculated using | |
	Equation (5.5)	Monte Carlo simulation
A	12,218	9922
B	6012	5669
C	86.9	92.0
D	1561	2025

TABLE 16. ACCURACY OF APPROXIMATE
APPROACH TO ESTIMATING THE
STANDARD DEVIATION OF IRR

| Case study | Standard deviation of IRR calculated using | |
	Equation (5.5)	Monte Carlo simulation
A	26.9	22.5
D	1.1	1.5

The results produced do strongly suggest that, if variables are independent, in order to get an approximate measure of the standard deviation of the performance measure it is only necessary for a company to:

(a) provide the estimates U_j, L_j and E_j for each variable: and

(b) estimate $k_j = \dfrac{\sigma_j}{U_j - L_j}$ for each variable j.

Estimating the k_j is not straightforward but some guidance can be obtained from work which has been carried out in connection with the use of PERT. Malcolm *et al.* (1959) on the basis of an examination of the beta distribution suggest that if L_j and U_j correspond to 0% and 100% fractiles of the distribution it is reasonable to assume:

$$k_j = \frac{1}{6}.$$

Moder and Rogers (1968) more realistically assume that L_j and U_j correspond to 0.05 and 0.95 fractiles and suggest, again on the basis of the beta distribution, that $k_j = 0.31$. In fact, if a normal distribution is assumed for the variable, it is a straightforward matter to calculate the values of k_j which correspond to different interpretations of L_j and U_j. This has been done in Table 17.

TABLE 17. VALUES OF k_j FOR DIFFERENT
INTERPRETATIONS OF L_j AND U_j
ASSUMING A NORMAL DISTRIBUTION

Fractile to which L_j corresponds	0.05	0.10	0.20
Fractile to which U_j corresponds	0.95	0.90	0.80
Value of k_j	0.30	0.39	0.59

Reasonable rules of thumb are to set k_j equal to 0.3 when L_j and U_j correspond to 0.05 and 0.95 fractiles, and to set $k_j = 0.4$ when L_j and U_j correspond to 0.10 and 0.90 fractiles.

One point worth noting is that, whatever the definition of optimistic and pessimistic estimates, $\sqrt{\sum_j S_j^2}$ is an estimate of the difference between the optimistic and pessimistic NPV.

5.6. Approximating to the Mean of the Performance Measure

At this stage it is appropriate to say a few words about how an estimate of μ_p can be obtained.

The most natural approach towards obtaining a "best estimate" of the performance measure is to combine together best estimates of the individual variables, i.e. to calculate

$$f(E_1, E_2 \ldots E_m).$$

However an examination of the case studies described in Section 5.4 shows that this can lead to severe errors when some distributions are skewed. This is because the best estimate of a variable corresponds to its mode (not to its mean) and modes are not well behaved algebraically.

Ideally, the analyst should obtain estimates of the means of variables. These should then be combined together to form μ_p. In other words the formula:

$$\mu_p = f(\mu_1, \mu_2 \ldots \mu_m). \qquad (5.6)$$

should always be used in preference to the formula:

$$\mu_p = f(E_1, E_2 \ldots E_m). \qquad (5.7)$$

Table 18 summarises the difference this can make for the four case studies where P is net present value.

TABLE 18. ADVANTAGE OF EQUATION (5.6)
OVER EQUATION (5.7) FOR THE
FIVE CASE STUDIES

	True mean	Mean given by Equation 5.6	Mean given by Equation 5.7
Case A	-2590	-2470	5880
Case B	1750	2130	5670
Case C	71	57	60
Case D	2980	3170	2260

The mean of a skewed variable is not something which is cognitively easy for the individual to estimate directly, and one approach is to use the well tried PERT formula:

$$\mu_j = \frac{1}{6}(L_j + 4E_j + U_j). \qquad (5.8)$$

The assumption that μ_p and σ_p are the only aspects of the distribution of the performance measure which are of interest to management is not necessarily a valid one. μ_p and σ_p will often be the two most important parameters of P — particularly in view of the results in Hull (1977) which strongly suggest that, in practice, the distribution of P can often be expected to be approximately normal. At the very least it can be said that estimates for μ_p and σ_p would form a good basis for a preliminary screening of investment opportunities.

5.7. The Importance of Different Features of the Input Variables

In section 5.3 it was shown that for a linear model:
(i) the effect of an error in the mean of variable j on the mean of NPV is

equal to $p_j S_j$ where p_j is equal to the error expressed as a fraction of the range of the variable;

(ii) the effect of a certain error in the standard deviation of variable j on the standard deviation of the performance measure is approximately

$$\frac{S_j^2 \, q_j \, k_j^2}{\sigma_p}$$

where q_j is the error expressed as a fraction of σ_j.

In order to test these results on a non linear model, eighteen simulations were carried out for case A using NPV as the performance and a discount of 10%. The first nine simulations involved testing the effect of increasing the mean of each of the nine variables in the model by 5% of the variable's range while keeping the standard deviation fixed. The other nine simulations tested the effect of increasing the standard deviation of each of the nine variables by 30% while keeping the mean fixed. The results are shown in Table 19.

The table shows that the results produced for the linear model do hold approximately for case A (Note that when testing the second result the estimate of σ_p produced in Section 5.5 was used.) One note of caution should be sounded. In a non-linear model it is possible for an error in μ_j to have an effect on σ_p and for an error in σ_j to have an effect on μ_p. The S_js are *not* good predictors of the extent of these effects. Generally, the effect of an

TABLE 19. SENSITIVITY COEFFICIENTS AS ESTIMATORS OF THE
EFFECTS OF ERRORS IN MEANS AND STANDARD DEVIATIONS
FOR HERTZ MODEL

Variable	Effect on μ_p of increase in means equal to 5% of range		Effect on σ_j of 30% increase in standard deviation	
	Actual	Estimated	Actual	Estimated
Initial market size	+349	+743	+201	+231
Market growth	+83	+179	+27	+13
Selling price	+1626	+1962	+1591	+1627
Market share	+457	+903	+295	+343
Initial investment	−175	−175	+12	+13
Life of investment	+107	+414	+10	+70
Residual value	+27	+29	+2	0
Operating costs	−1498	−1807	+1280	+1366
Fixed costs	−39	−38	−1	+1

TABLE 20. EFFECTS OF ERRORS IN MEAN ON
STANDARD DEVIATION OF NPV

Variable	Effect on σ_p of increase in mean equal to 5% of range
Initial market size	+464
Market growth	+121
Selling price	+177
Market share	+579
Initial investment	0
Life of investment	+316
Residual value	0
Operating costs	+131
Fixed costs	0

error in σ_j on μ_p will be small. But the effect of an error in μ_j on σ_p can be quite large as indicated in Table 20.

As far as dependencies between variables are concerned, it was shown in Section 5.3 that, for a linear model, the effect of a coefficient of correlation ρ_{jk} between variables j and k on σ_p is approximately:

$$\frac{S_j \ S_k \ k_j \ k_k \ \rho_{jk}}{\sigma_p}$$

An examination of results produced for case A (see Table 10) reveals that this formula is not an unreasonable approximation for that case study. Once again a note of caution must be sounded. For a non-linear model a dependence between two variables is liable to affect μ_p. The magnitudes of S_j and S_k do not provide a good indication as to the extent of this effect.

5.8. Potential Pitfalls

Although many of the results obtained assuming a linear model have been found to apply approximately in the case of the non-linear models which have been considered, it is worth pointing out that, in theory, the results from a sensitivity analysis can be *totally* misleading and that the analyst should be aware of potential pitfalls.

Suppose

$$P = X_1 X_2 + X_3$$

with $\sigma_j = 4$ for all j and:

$$
\begin{array}{lll}
L_1 = -11 & E_1 = 1 & U_1 = 13 \\
L_2 = -12 & E_2 = 0 & U_2 = 12 \\
L_3 = 0 & E_3 = 12 & U_3 = 24
\end{array}
$$

with the distributions of the three variables being independent. Then it is easy to see that

$$
\begin{array}{l}
S_1 = 0 \\
S_2 = 24 \\
S_3 = 24
\end{array}
$$

giving the impression that errors in the distribution of X_1 are totally unimportant when compared with errors in the distributions of X_2 and X_3, and that errors in the distributions of X_2 and X_3 are equally important. It can be shown that a small percentage error in σ_1 has sixteen times the effect on σ_p as the same percentage error in σ_3 and only marginally less effect than the same percentage error in σ_2.

Another example of a situation where the results from a sensitivity analysis can be misleading is the situation where a company is manufacturing a product for two markets: market I and market II, and

(a) market II will only be supplied if market I has been completely satisfied, and

(b) on the basis of best estimates market I cannot be completely satisfied.

A sensitivity analysis would then produce the result: $S_j = 0$ for all variables j relating to market II even though there might be a high probability of market II being supplied (This situation is fairly similar to that existing in the case study which is examined in Chapter 8, although in that case a fuller analysis showed that the variables connected with the second market were not important).

5.9. Reducing the Number of Probability Assessments to a Minimum

If it is decided to carry out a risk simulation in a given situation, the analyst must keep to a minimum the total number of probability assessments which management are asked to make. This section will explore the way in which the research described in this chapter can help as far as this is concerned.

If there are m variables in a particular situation, the chapter indicates that the proportion of the overall uncertainty in the performance measure (or to be more precise the proportion of σ_p^2) which is accounted for by the k most sensitive variables, is approximately:

$$\frac{\sum\limits_{j=1}^{k} S_j^2}{\sum\limits_{j=1}^{m} S_j^2}$$

Usually, this will be close to unity for a relatively small value of k, say $k = K$. This is encouraging as it suggests that the analyst need only asssess distributions for a small number, K, of the variables with the remainder of the variables being assumed to be fixed at estimates of their mean. There are just three notes of caution as far as this is concerned.

(i) Non-linearities in the model may reduce the proportion of the total uncertainty accounted for by the k most sensitive variables.

(ii) The accuracy of μ_p depends to a large extent on the accuracy of the μ_js and the effect on μ_p of a certain error in μ_j is governed by the magnitude of S_j — not S_j^2. It may, therefore, be justifiable to assess a distribution for variable j in order to improve the estimate of μ_j and hence the estimate of μ_p.

(iii) If a moderately sensitive variable is not described by a distribution, there is a possibility that an important dependence between that variable and a highly sensitive variable will be overlooked.

Sometimes it may be considered desirable to carry out an exploratory "test" risk simulation without any detailed probability distributions being assessed. One way of proceeding involves choosing sampling distributions which have means and standard deviations corresponding to PERT estimates of the means and standard deviations of the variables. Triangular distributions being particularly easy (and cheap in terms of computer time) to sample from (as well as being bounded) are useful distributions in this context. Suppose that the estimates of the mean and standard deviation of variable j are μ_j and σ_j. If a_j, b_j and m_j are the lower bound, upper bound and mode of the triangular distribution used to describe variable j, then

$$\mu_j = \frac{1}{3}\,(a_j + m_j + b_j)$$

$$\sigma_j^2 = \frac{(b_j - a_j)^2 + (m_j - a_j)\,(m_j - b_j)}{18}$$

If we impose the condition

$$\frac{b_j - m_j}{m_j - a_j} = \frac{U_j - E_j}{E_j - L_j} = \phi \text{ say}$$

then it can be shown that

$$m_j = \mu_j - \frac{1}{3}\,\psi\,(\phi - 1)$$

$$a_j = m_j - \psi$$

$$b_j = m_j + \psi\phi$$

where

$$\psi = \sigma_j \sqrt{\frac{18}{1 + \phi + \phi^2}}$$

Appendix B includes subroutines to carry out these calculations.

5.10. Summary and Conclusions

This chapter has suggested a number of ways in which a company can derive a great deal of information from relatively simple analyses based on optimistic, pessimistic and most likely estimates for the variables.

The most interesting results in this chapter concern the calculation of estimates for μ_p and σ_p. Very little effort over and above that expended in carrying out an ordinary sensitivity analysis is involved in producing the estimates. (The computer program for carrying out sensitivity analyses which is described in Appendix A produces them automatically.) Often the accept/reject decision will be clear from the estimates. For example, suppose that the management's normal criteria for accepting investments amounts to "accept if the probability of a positive NPV is greater than 0.9". If μ_p and σ_p were estimated at 5000 and 500 respectively it would seem reasonable to assume that the investment satisfied the criterion. The analyst would wish to inspect the model carefully to satisfy himself that it had no unusual features; possibly he would wish to carry out a test risk simulation along the lines described in the previous section. However, it is likely that he would manage to avoid having to ask management for any detailed probability assessments.

The extent to which a particular probability assessment (or group of probability assessments) is worth obtaining must be judged on the basis of the extent to which it could cause the accept/reject decision on the investment to change. The results produced for the linear model provide a useful guide as far as this is concerned. Suppose that a variable has a sensitivity coefficient of 10,000 and that σ_p is estimated as approximately 100,000. Suppose further that it is considered that making detailed probability assessments for the variable could:

(a) change the current estimate of its mean by as much as 5% of its range (but probably by no more than this);

(b) change the current estimate of its standard deviation by as much as 40% (but probably by no more than this).

The results in Section 5.3 suggest that the maximum likely change to μ_p arising from the extra assessments is 500, and that the maximum likely change to σ_p arising from the extra assessments would be 36. (This assumes a standard deviation to range ratio of 0.3.)

Sometimes the sensitivity coefficient of one variable will be very much greater than that of all other variables. In such cases there is almost certainly no need for a risk simulation. The probability of the performance measure exceeding a certain value will equal the probability of the sensitive variable exceeding a corresponding value.

References

ECONOMOS, A. M. (1968). A financial simulation for risk analysis of a proposed subsidiary, *Management Science*, vol. 15, B, no. 12, pp. 675-82.

HERTZ, D. B. (1964). Risk analysis in capital investment, *Harvard Business Review*, Jan.-Feb., pp. 95-106.

HULL, J. C. (1977). The inputs to and outputs from risk evaluation models, *European Journal of Operational Research*, vol. 1, pp. 368-75.

HULL, J. C. (1978). The interpretation of the output from a sensitivity analysis in investment appraisal, *Journal of Business Finance and Accounting*, vol. 5, no. 1, pp. 109-21.

KRYZANOWSKI, L., LUSZTIG, P. and SCHWAB, B. (1972). Monte Carlo simulation and capital expenditure decisions — a case study, *Engineering Economist,* vol. 18, no. 1, pp. 31–47.
MALCOLM, D. G., ROSEBOOM, J. H. CLARK, C. E. and FAZAR, W. (1959). Application of a technique for research and development program evaluation, *Operations Research,* vol. 7, no. 5, pp. 646–69.
MODER, J. J. and ROGERS, E. G. (1968). Judgement estimates of the moments of PERT type distributions, *Management Science,* vol. 15, B, no. 2, pp. 76–83.
VANDELL, R. F. (1970). *Interchemical Consumer Products,* Case Clearing House of Great Britain and Ireland, Ref. ICH9-271-621.

Chapter 6
SEQUENTIAL INVESTMENT DECISIONS

6.1. Introduction

So far, we have restricted our attention to the evaluation of the risk in investment projects where, at the outset, management must make a single accept/reject decision. In this chapter we will consider what are usually termed sequential investment decision situations — that is, situations where several decisions on an investment have to be made over a period of time. The basic decision-tree methodology will be presented, and the way in which it can be used in conjunction with the risk evaluation procedures described elsewhere in this book will be examined. An investment project often involves sequential decisions because the possibility of abandoning the project exists at various points during its life. The nature of the abandonment option and the effect of abandonment options on a project's expected return and risk will be given particular attention.

6.2. Decisions and Outcomes

At the outset of this chapter it is appropriate to stress the distinction between decision variables and outcome variables. Decision variables are under the control of management; outcome variables are not. In a risk evaluation, outcome variables need to be described probabilistically; decision variables should not be so described.

This may seem an obvious observation but it should be noted that there can be arguments about the status of a particular variable. Consider again the Hertz case study. The variable "unit price" is an outcome variable described by a probability distribution. Presumably this is because Hertz considered that price was determined by overall market conditions. It is easy to imagine other situations in which unit price would be a decision variable under the control of management. In such situations there would, in effect, be several investment projects under consideration by the company, e.g.

Go ahead with a high unit price.
Go ahead with a medium unit price.
Go ahead with a low unit price.

Each project would have to be evaluated separately. The estimates made for some variables would be the same, regardless of the price, but it is likely that other variables such as market share would have to be considered separately for each unit price under consideration. If there were the extra complication of management being able to change their pricing strategy mid-stream, then the methods described in this chapter would become appropriate.

6.3. The Decision-Tree Methodology

A decision-tree is essentially a diagram for displaying the different sequences of decisions and outcomes which can occur in a given situation. To illustrate the basic idea, consider a company which has to decide whether to invest £100,000 in a 1 year R and D project aimed at developing a special new product. If the project is successful then the company can choose between building a plant capable of producing 100,000 units per annum, and one capable of producing 200,000 units per annum.

Figure XIII shows a decision tree describing the situation facing the company. There are two sorts of nodes on the tree. The rectangular-shaped nodes (■) are known as decision nodes. They represent points in time where a choice has to be made between alternative courses of action. The circular nodes (●) are known as outcome nodes. They represent points in time where events outside the control of the decision-maker happen.

In Fig. XIII, the first node is a decision node and the two branches emanating from the node indicate that the company can either go ahead or not go ahead with the R and D programme. If it does not go ahead no further decisions and outcomes are important. (Hence the "not go ahead with R and D" branch leads to no further branches.) If the company goes ahead with the R and D, the tree shows that there are two possible outcomes: "R and D successful" and "R and D unsuccessful". If the R and

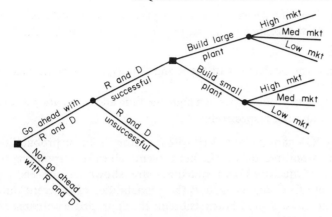

FIGURE XIII. Example of decision tree

D is unsuccessful we are again in the situation where there are no further relevant decisions or outcomes. If the programme is successful the company must, as the second decision node on the tree shows, choose between a large plant and a small plant. Whichever decision is taken the final branches on the tree show that the market size is liable to be "high", "medium" or "low".

In order to analyse a decision tree, it is necessary to calculate a net present value (or some other suitable performance measure) corresponding to each possible sequence of decisions and outcomes. In Fig. XIII there are a total of eight such sequences and we shall assume:

(a) that the present value of the cost of the R and D programme is £100,000;

(b) that the cost in present value terms of a small plant is £200,000 and of a large plant is £400,000;

(c) that a small plant can cope with a low or medium market size, but not with a high market size;

(d) that the present value of the cash flows corresponding to sales to a high market, medium market and low market over the life of the plant are £1,000,000, £500,000 and £250,000 respectively.

An analysis of a decision tree also requires that probabilities be assigned to each of the branches emanating from an outcome node. We shall assume:

(a) that the probability of the R and D programme being successful is 0.6;

(b) that the probabilities of a high, medium and low market size are 0.5, 0.3 and 0.2 respectively.

Figure XIV shows Figure XIII with the information on probabilities and NPVs incorporated on it. The net present values corresponding to each sequence of decisions and outcomes are shown at the ends of the appropriate final branches, and the probabilities of different outcomes happening are shown in brackets beside the appropriate outcome branch.

Once Fig. XIV has been drawn, a procedure which is illustrated in Fig. XV and is known as roll back can begin. This assumes that the company wishes to maximise expected NPV, and involves working from the right of the tree to the left asking at each node (decision node or outcome node) the question: "How much is it worth to be at this node?"

The first nodes encountered in the decision tree under consideration are (see Fig. XV) nodes D and E. If we are at node D the tree indicates that

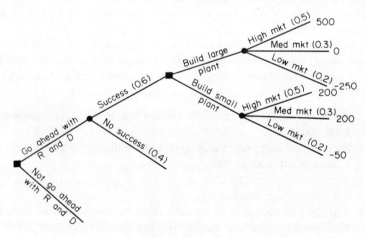

FIG. XIV Decision tree with probabilities and NPVs (NPVs in £'000s)

there is a 0.5 probability of (in £'000s) an NPV of £500, a 0.3 probability of 0 and a 0.2 probability of –250. Hence the expected NPV if node D is reached is (in £'000s):

$$0.5 \times 500 + 0.3 \times 0 + 0.2 \times (-250) = 200.$$

(This value is shown adjacent to node D in Fig. XV.) Similarly, the expected NPV if node E is reached is:

$$0.5 \times 200 + 0.3 \times 200 + 0.2 \times (-50) = 150.$$

Now consider node C. Node C is a decision node. If we reach it we can choose whether we move to node D where the expected NPV is 200 or node E where the expected NPV is 150. Given that the basic assumption underlying the analysis is that we wish to maximise expected NPV we will choose the former. Hence the expected NPV associated with node C is 200.

Consider next node B. At this node there is an 0.6 probability of reaching a point where the expected NPV is 200 and an 0.4 probability of reaching a point where it is – 100. Hence the expected NPV associated with node B is 80 and as this is better than zero it is also the expected NPV associated with node A.

It will by now be apparent that decision trees are really just a

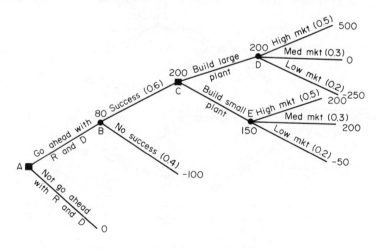

FIG. XV. The roll back procedure (NPVs in £'000s)

straightforward way of describing a sequential decision situation and applying the "maximise expected NPV" decision criterion. In the example examined we have shown that the criterion implies that it is best to go ahead with the R and D programme and that the expected NPV from doing so is £80,000.

6.4.   The Expected Value of Perfect Information

We now carry the example just considered a little further by supposing that the company can buy market research information on the size of the market. Most information of this sort is imperfect in that it does not make us completely certain about something we were previously uncertain about. However, it is often useful to imagine that perfect information can be bought at no cost and then observe the resultant increase in expected NPV. This is what we do here.

Figure XVI shows an extra branch of the decision tree drawn on the assumption that perfect information is immediately available. Note that because the probabilities of high, medium and low market sizes are 0.5, 0.3

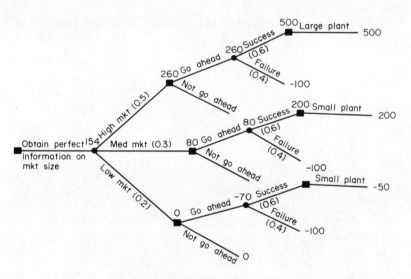

FIG. XVI. Calculating the value of perfect information

and 0.2 respectively, these must also be the probabilities of perfect information telling the company that there will be high, medium and low market sizes. A roll back analysis shows (see Fig. XVI) that the company's expected NPV in the new situation is £154,000. The difference between this and the company's previous expected NPV of £80,000 is £74,000. Therefore, £74,000 does represent the expected value of perfect information. It is a measure of the maximum price the company should be prepared to pay for market research information. It is the maximum amount by which extra information on market size can increase expected NPV. If the information costs more than £74,000, however good it is, it cannot be worth it!

An expected value of perfect information corresponding to any of the uncertainties in a given situation can be calculated. In the example which has just been considered it is easy to show that the expected value of perfect information on whether the R and D programme will be successful is £40,000. (This has a simple interpretation: there is a 40% chance of the information saving the company £100,000.)

The expected value of perfect information analysis is a quick analysis which can be useful in a wide variety of situations. A manager's natural inclination is always to collect as much data as possible before making any decision. This can be very wasteful if the data is expensive or if the chance of it causing him to change his decision is very small.

6.5. Bayesian Analysis

If a detailed study of the situation where a firm has the option to buy imperfect information is required, a form of analysis known as "Bayesian" may be appropriate.

Suppose in the example which has been considered, that the firm can, at a cost of £50,000, carry out a quick market survey which would either give a "favourable" or an "unfavourable" result. The decision tree corresponding to this new situation is shown in Fig. XVII. In order to carry out the roll-back analysis it is clear from the figure that we need to know:

Prob (F), Prob (U)
Prob (H/F), Prob (M/F), Prob (L/F)
Prob (H/U), Prob (M/U), Prob (L/U)

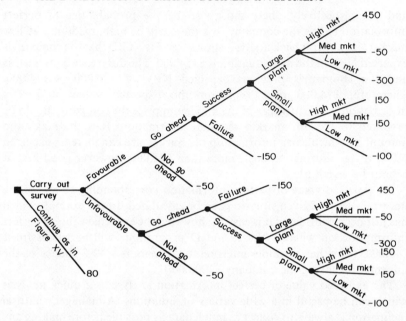

FIG. XVII. Decision tree on the assumption that a quick market survey can be carried out

where F and U stand for "favourable result from survey" and "unfavourable result from survey", and H, M and L stand for high, medium and low market size. Using the normal notation of probability theory, Prob (X/Y) means the probability of X happening given that Y has happened. Thus Prob (H/F) is the probability of sales being high given a favourable survey result. The eight probabilities could be assessed individually but there would then be the problem that they might not be consistent with Prob (H), Prob (M) and Prob (L) which are known to be 0.5, 0.3 and 0.2 respectively. For consistency it is true from elementary probability theory that:

$$\text{Prob (H)} = \text{Prob (H/F) Prob (F)} + \text{Prob (H/U) Prob (U)}$$
$$\text{Prob (M)} = \text{Prob (M/F) Prob (F)} + \text{Prob (M/U) Prob (U)}$$
$$\text{Prob (L)} = \text{Prob (L/F) Prob (F)} + \text{Prob (L/U) Prob (U)}.$$

The Bayesian approach to the problem involves asking management to assess:

$$\text{Prob (F/H); Prob (U/H)}$$
$$\text{Prob (F/M); Prob (U/M)}$$
$$\text{Prob (F/L); Prob (U/L).}$$

Prob (F) and Prob (U) can then be calculated from the formulae:

Prob (F) = Prob (F/H) Prob (H) + Prob (F/M) Prob (M) + Prob (F/L) Prob (L)

Prob (U) = Prob (U/H) Prob (H) + Prob (U/M) Prob (M) + Prob (U/L) Prob (L)

and the remaining probabilities which are required can be calculated from formulae such as

$$\text{Prob (H/F)} = \frac{\text{Prob (H) Prob (F/H)}}{\text{Prob (F)}}$$

Suppose that the assessments which are made are:

$$\text{Prob (F/H)} = 0.9; \text{Prob (U/H)} = 0.1$$
$$\text{Prob (F/M)} = 0.5; \text{Prob (U/M)} = 0.5$$
$$\text{Prob (F/L)} = 0.2; \text{Prob (U/L)} = 0.8.$$

It is easy to show by using the above formulae and a roll-back analysis on Fig. XVII that the expected NPV if the survey is carried out is approximately £58,200. This compares unfavourably with the company's expected NPV if the survey is not carried out. In other words the survey information is not worth £50,000.

6.6. Discussion of the Decision-Tree Methodology

Decision trees are a valuable way of breaking down a highly complex decision problem into a number of simpler ones and, as we have seen in the last two sections, they provide a useful vehicle for examining the value of extra information to the decision-maker.

One drawback to the decision-tree methodology, as it has been described so far, is the implicit assumption that the appropriate decision criteria is "maximise expected NPV". This assumption ignores the fact that most companies are, to a greater or lesser extent, risk averse. In Chapter 7 we shall see how a company's attitudes to risk can be taken into account by using utility theory. Sometimes it is more useful simply to display a distribution of NPV for different decision strategies.

One approach to obtaining a distribution of NPV corresponding to a particular decision strategy, involves a straightforward analysis of the probabilities on the tree. To illustrate the general idea let us return to the decision tree which was considered in Section 6.3. The "best" decision strategy was identified as: go ahead with the R and D programme and if this is successful build a large plant. If this strategy is followed an inspection of Fig. XV shows that:

(a) there is a 0.4 probability of an NPV of –£100,000;
(b) there is a 0.6 × 0.2 = 0.12 probability of an NPV of –£250,000;
(c) there is a 0.6 × 0.3 = 0.18 probability of an NPV of 0;
(d) there is a 0.6 × 0.5 = 0.3 probability of an NPV of £500,000.

In other words, the situation is as summarised in Table 21. Although the expected NPV is £80,000 it can be seen that the decision strategy is clearly quite risky.

TABLE 21.
PROBABILITY
DISTRIBUTION OF
NPV WHICH CAN BE
CALCULATED
ARITHMETICALLY
FROM FIG. XV.

NPV (£'000s)	Probability
–250	0.12
–100	0.4
0	0.18
+500	0.30

The probability distribution in Table 21 can, at best, be regarded as approximate because of the assumptions which went into the construction of the tree in Fig. XV. Only two different plant sizes ànd three different market sizes were considered. Furthermore, other variables such as fixed costs per annum, variable costs of production, price, etc., were assumed to be known for certain. Any analysis of any investment decision is going to involve some discretisation of alternative decisions and alternative outcomes. However, it is important to make the point that a decision tree can require quite drastic assumptions if the analytic approach which has been described is to be at all manageable. If the Hertz model was displayed on a decision tree with three different values of each of the nine outcome variables being considered, then 3^9 (= 19683) different paths through the tree would have to be evaluated, and if five different values of each variable were considered then the total number of paths through the tree would be nearly 2M!

An alternative to the analytic approach for evaluating decision trees is simulation. Hespos and Strassman (1965) were the first to suggest that the risk simulation methodology and the decision tree methodology can be combined. Their basic idea is very simple. First, it is necessary for management to assess probability distributions corresponding to each of the uncertainties in a sequential decision situation. Several different good decision strategies are then defined using a decision tree in the usual way and Monte Carlo simulation is used to evaluate them. The simulation is liable to be somewhat more complicated than that for a straightforward investment in that decisions taken at various points during the investment's life may depend on values sampled from the probability distributions. It is worth noting that the simulation approach can incorporate a Bayesian analysis. Consider the example in Section 6.5. Management could first assess a distribution for market size and then a series of conditional distributions for survey results. The analysis would be arranged so that the market-size distribution was sampled from first — even though it is the results of the survey which are logically required first. The need for inverting the conditionality in the assessed distributions in the way described in Section 6.5 is therefore avoided when a simulation is carried out.

6.7. Abandonment Options

An investment project is usually analysed under the assumption that the company is committed to the project for its entire estimated life. This can lead to misleading results. Many projects have significant abandonment values over their economic lives and a recognition of the possibility of abandonment may increase a project's expected return as well as reducing its risk.

If the "maximise expected NPV" decision rule is used, then it is clear that a project should be abandoned when its abandonment value (i.e. its net disposal value) exceeds the NPV of the project's expected future cash flows. Generally this would seem to be a good working rule to incorporate into any analysis. It is appreciated that many risk averse companies might choose to abandon when the abandonment value is slightly less than the NPV of the project's expected future cash flows. However, this is a "second order effect" and is not likely to affect the project's overall expected return or risk to any great extent.

Van Horne (1977) considers a simple example which illustrates the potential importance of the abandonment option. An investment proposal costs $3000 initially and is expected to generate cash flows over 2 years in the way indicated in Table 22. The proposal has a residual value of $1500 at the end of the first year and zero at the end of the second year. There are nine possible series of cash flows over the 2-year period, the first series representing a cash flow of $1000 in year 1 followed by zero in year 2 with a probability of $0.25 \times 0.25 = 0.0625$.

If a discount rate of 10% is assumed and no abandonment is allowed, the

TABLE 22. PROBABILITY DISTRIBUTIONS FOR
VAN HORNE'S EXAMPLE

Year 1		Year 2		
Cash flow ($)	Probability	Cash flow ($)	Conditional probability	Joint probability
		0	0.25	0.0625
1000	0.25	1000	0.50	0.1250
		2000	0.25	0.0625
		1000	0.25	0.1250
2000	0.50	2000	0.50	0.2500
		3000	0.25	0.1250
		2000	0.25	0.0625
3000	0.25	3000	0.50	0.1250
		3500	0.25	0.0625

expected value and standard deviation of NPV can easily be calculated to be $444 and $1313 respectively from Table 22.

If abandonment is allowed, then it is necessary to consider carefully the position at the end of year 1. If the cash flow in year 1 is $1000 then the project should be abandoned at the end of year 1 because the NPV of the expected cash flow in year 2 is then $909 and this is less than the abandonment value of $1500. However, if the cash flow in year 1 is $2000 or $3000 the project should not be abandoned. The position is as summarised in Table 23. For the first alternative, the cash flow has for year 1 become $2500, the sum of $1000 for the year 1 cash flow and the abandonment value of $1500.

TABLE 23. VAN HORNE'S EXAMPLE WITH
ABANDONMENT OPTIONS

Year 1		Year 2		
Cash flow ($)	Probability	Cash flow ($)	Conditional probability	Joint probability
2500	0.25	0	1.0	0.2500
		1000	0.25	0.1250
2000	0.50	2000	0.50	0.2500
		3000	0.25	0.1250
		2000	0.25	0.0625
3000	0.25	3000	0.50	0.1250
		3500	0.25	0.0625

Calculations on the basis of the numbers in Table 23 show that, with abandonment, the project's expected NPV and standard deviation of NPV are $578 and $1110 respectively. Thus the effect of incorporating the abandonment option has been to increase the expected NPV by $134 and reduce the standard deviation of NPV by $203. These results are both due to the fact that a portion of the downside risk has been eliminated.

Robichek and Van Horne (1967) give an example of the use of simulation to solve the abandonment problem in a project with a 10-year life. Their results are summarised in Table 24. Again we see that the effect of abandonment options is to increase the expected NPV and to reduce the standard deviation of NPV. The skewness measure is the ratio of the

TABLE 24. RESULTS FOR EXAMPLE CONSIDERED IN ROBICHEK
AND VAN HORNE (1967)

		Without abandonment	With abandonment
NPV:	Expected value	672	991
	Standard deviation	1422	888
	Skewness	1.01	2.96
IRR:	Expected value	9.83	13.62
	Standard deviation	5.31	2.25
	Skewness	0.75	1.25

variance to twice the semi-variance. It equals 1.0 for a symmetrical distribution and increases as the distribution becomes more positively skewed. The measure shows clearly the extent to which abandonment options reduce the downside risk.

6.8.　Summary

Decision trees are a useful first step in the evaluation of a sequential investment decision. They enable alternative courses of action to be considered in a systematic and logical way, while at the same time providing a means by which the value of extra information to the decision-maker can be analysed. There are, however, two major drawbacks to the basic decision-tree methodology:

(i) A decision criterion such as "maximise expected NPV" must be defined and included in the analysis.

(ii) Only a restricted number of different values of the decision variables and outcome variables can be considered — as otherwise the analysis may get out of hand.

It is therefore suggested that the decision tree be used to identify a number of potentially good decision strategies and that the methods described in this book be used to evaluate more fully the distributions of NPV associated with the strategies.

An investment decision where there are abandonment options is, in effect, a sequential decision and can be handled in the way which has just been described. The importance of the abandonment options will naturally depend on the type of investment under consideration. If the investment is in a multi-purpose plant in a large city its abandonment value is likely to be quite high; on the other hand, if the plant is an inflexible one situated in the middle of nowhere abandonment options are probably not worth considering. Generally, the effect of an abandonment option is to increase the expected value of NPV, reduce its standard deviation and reduce the downside risk.

References

HESPOS, R. F. and STRASSMAN, P. A. (1965). Stochastic decision trees for the analysis of investment decisions, *Management Science*, B, vol. 11, no. 10, pp. 244–59.
ROBICHEK, A. A. and VAN HORNE, J. C. (1967). Abandonment value and capital budgeting, *Journal of Finance*, vol. 22, no. 4, pp. 577–89.
VAN HORNE, J. C. (1977). *Financial Management and Policy*, 4th edn., Prentice Hall.

Chapter 7
RISK AND RETURN — SOME THEORETICAL IDEAS

7.1. Introduction

This chapter presents a number of theoretical ideas concerned with the risk and return from an investment project. It starts by showing how modern utility theory provides a framework within which trade offs between the total risk and total return can be made. It then goes on to show that the marginal risk to a company of embarking on an individual investment project can depend to a considerable extent on the other investment projects which the company has undertaken or is about to undertake. Finally, the viewpoint of one of the company's shareholders is considered; the capital asset pricing model is described and its relevance to the capital investment decision is explained.

7.2. Utility Theory

A theoretical framework comparing any uncertain outcomes (not necessarily those arising from investment decisions) is provided by utility theory as developed in von Neumann and Morgenstern (1947). The theory starts with a number of fairly reasonable axioms of rational behaviour such as:

(i) Individuals are always able to rank outcomes in preference order.
(ii) If outcome A is preferred to outcome B and outcome B is preferred to outcome C then outcome A is preferred to outcome C.
(iii) For any uncertain outcome there is a certainty equivalent. For example, if an individual has a 50% chance of receiving £1000 and a 50% chance of receiving nothing then there is a certain sum of

money, say £X, between £0 and £1000 which is such that he is indifferent between £X and the gamble.

The theory then goes on to show that the axioms lead to the existence of a utility function, u, with the following properties:

(a) u is defined on the set of all possible outcomes;
(b) outcome A is preferred to outcome B if and only if $u(A) > u(B)$;
(c) a decision giving chances p_i of achieving outcomes A_i ($1 \leqslant i \leqslant n$) is preferred to one giving chances q_j of achieving outcomes B_j ($1 \leqslant j \leqslant m$) where

$$\sum_{i=1}^{n} p_i = \sum_{j=1}^{m} q_j = 1$$

if and only if

$$\sum_{i=1}^{n} p_i u(A_i) > \sum_{j=1}^{m} q_j u(B_j).$$

Property (b) shows that a utility function ranks the outcomes in preference order while property (c) shows that one set of probabilistic outcomes is preferred to another if, and only if, it has a higher expected utility. It follows from property (c) that a "rational" man will always act so as to maximise his expected utility.

The outcomes from investment projects are usually described in terms of NPVs or IRRs. However, the reader will best appreciate the ideas of utility theory if he attempts to obtain his own personal utility scale for outcomes which correspond to a straightforward gain of sums of money between, say, £0 and £5000. The first stage involves ascertaining what a 50:50 gamble on these two sums of money is worth. What would you sell such a gamble for? For £4000? Yes, you probably would! For £100? Probably not! Eventually you should obtain a sum of money, say £X, which is equivalent to a 50:50 gamble on £0 and £5000. If we suppose

$$u \text{ (gain £0)} = 0$$
$$u \text{ (gain £5000)} = 100$$

then

$$u \text{ (gain } \pounds X) = 0.5 \times 0 + 0.5 \times 100 = 50.$$

Similarly you can obtain a sum of money, say $\pounds Y$, equivalent to a 50:50 gamble on $\pounds 0$ and $\pounds X$ and also a sum of money, say $\pounds Z$, equivalent to a 50:50 gamble on $\pounds X$ and $\pounds 5000$. It is easy to see that

$$u \text{ (gain } \pounds Y) = 25$$
$$u \text{ (gain } \pounds Z) = 75.$$

If $X = 1000$, $Y = 400$ and $Z = 2250$ the utility curve shown in Fig. XVIII would then be obtained. The concave shape of the curve is an indication of risk aversion.

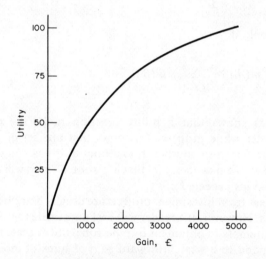

FIG. XVIII. Utility curve

Returning to a consideration of investment decisions, utility theory implies that a company should maximise expected utility not expected NPV. In decision trees, for example, it is the utilities of different NPVs — not the NPVs themselves — which should be put on the ends of the final branches.

In practice, determining a curve similar to that shown in Fig. XVIII, relating utilities to NPVs, is not easy. One problem is the nature of the questions which management must answer (e.g. Is an NPV of +£1000 preferable to a 50:50 chance of NPVs of −£2000 and +£5000?). Another problem is deciding whether the questions should be answered by an individual manager or by a group of managers representing the company. In many situations it is reasonable to conjecture that the individual manager with responsibilities for an investment will be more risk averse than the company as a whole because, if the investment goes badly, his job may be at stake. Hull *et al.* (1973) provides a discussion of the problems in measuring utility, while studies aimed at obtaining utility functions for practising businessmen are described in Grayson (1960), Green (1963), Cramer and Smith (1964), Swalm (1966) and Spetzler (1968).

Two points should be noted about utilities:

(i) There is no reason why two different people should have the same utilities for outcomes in a certain situation. Utilities are very much personal value judgements and are, in this respect, analogous to subjective probabilities.

(ii) A utility scale is not fixed until two points on it have been fixed. In this respect it is like a scale for measuring temperature. In Fig. XVIII, instead of defining u (gain £0) = 0 and u (gain £5000) = 100 we could equally well have defined u (gain £0) = 10 and u (gain £5000) = 20.

7.3. The Quadratic Utility Function

A number of authors have suggested that the functional form

$$u(P) = aP^2 + bP + c \qquad (7.1)$$

be assumed for the utility, u, of the performance measure, P, where a, b and c are constants with $a/b < 0$. This has the same general concave shape as the curve shown in Fig. XVIII. Furthermore,

$$E\,[u(P)] = a\,E(P^2) + b\,E(P) + c$$

where E denotes expected value. If μ and σ are the mean and standard deviation of P, since

$$\sigma^2 = E\,(P^2) - \mu^2,$$

it follows that

$$E\ [u(P)] = a\sigma^2 + a\mu^2 + b\mu + c.$$

This shows that, if a quadratic utility function is assumed, the expected utility of an investment depends only on the mean and the standard deviation of its performance measure. In other words, the quadratic utility function assumption implies that investment projects can be completely characterised by the means and standard deviations of their performance measures.

At the end of Section 7.2 it was pointed out that a utility scale — like a scale for measuring temperatures — needs two points to be defined on it. It follows from this that the quadratic utility function in Equation (7.1) is, in effect, describing attitudes to risk by a single parameter. All that management need do in order to determine the parameter is either provide a single certainty equivalent for a risky outcome, or provide a single indication of the nature of the trade-offs which can be made between μ and σ. Generally, the greater the absolute value of a/b, the greater the risk aversion which is being assumed by the utility function.

Pratt (1964) and Arrow (1965) have pointed out a weakness in the quadratic utility function assumption. They show that the quadratic utility function implies that investors become increasingly risk averse as their wealth increases — whereas common sense would suggest the reverse.

The theory in the rest of this chapter will assume that utility is a function of the mean and standard deviation of the performance measure only. This is a slightly less restrictive assumption than that implied by the quadratic utility function. (In fact, if it is assumed that the performance measure is always normally distributed the assumption is not restrictive at all.) The effect of the assumption is that a series of equi-utility curves such as those illustrated in Fig. XIX must exist.

7.4. Portfolios of Projects

Up to now we have confined our discussion to the evaluation of the risk in a single investment project. We now consider the relationship between the riskiness of a portfolio of investment projects and the riskiness of the individual projects comprising that portfolio.

Suppose that a company has an existing portfolio of projects with an

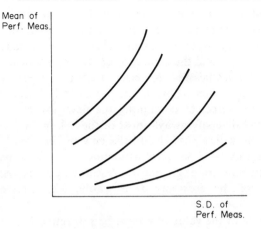

Mean of
Perf. Meas.

S.D. of
Perf. Meas.

FIG. XIX. Curves of equi-utility

NPV which has mean M and standard deviation S. Suppose further that the company is considering embarking on a new project whose NPV has mean μ and standard deviation σ. If it goes ahead with the project it follows from elementary statistics that the new portfolio's NPV will have mean M^* and standard deviation S^* given by:

$$M^* = M + \mu \qquad (7.2)$$
$$S^* = \sqrt{(S^2 + \sigma^2 + 2\rho S\sigma)} \qquad (7.3)$$

where ρ is the coefficient of correlation between the NPV of the existing portfolio and that of the new project.

Suppose that (in some suitable units) $\mu = 10$, $\sigma = 1$, $M = 100$ and $S = 10$. Equations (7.2) and (7.3) show that while M^* always equals 110, the value of S^* depends on ρ

if $\rho = 1$, $S^* = 11$
if $\rho = 0$, $S^* = 10.05$
if $\rho = -1$, $S^* = 9$.

This illustrates the nature of risk diversification for a company. The marginal effect of a new project on the overall riskiness of a company's portfolio depends critically on the extent to which the new project's returns are correlated with those of the portfolio. If the new project is very similar to others which the company has undertaken and can be expected to be affected by industry cycles, etc., in much the same way, then the value of ρ is probably close to 1 and the project offers few diversification advantages. (Equation (7.3) becomes $S^* = S + \sigma$ when $\rho = 1$). If the risk of the project is more or less independent of the risk in the rest of the business then ρ is close to zero and the effect of combining the new project with the existing portfolio is to "diversify away" most of the risk in the former. The ideal situation is one where $\rho = -1$ and the new project actually reduces the portfolio's risk ($S^* = S - \sigma$). Unfortunately, because the performances of most projects are to a greater or lesser extent correlated with the performance of the economy as a whole, high degrees of negative correlation are rare.

Any estimate of the value of ρ must be subjective. However, the above arguments show that it is crucially important that a company does attempt to get an estimate for ρ. Once the total risk of a project has been evaluated a company should ask questions such as: If our existing business does well how will this project tend to perform? If our existing business does badly how will this project tend to perform? In this way a rough guide as to the value of ρ can be obtained. Appendix C presents some theoretical ideas which can be used to make the analysis more rigorous.

In the literature a great deal of attention has been given to handling the portfolio investment decision problem in a formal way. Suppose that μ_j and σ_j are the mean and standard deviation of the jth project in a portfolio of m projects and that ρ_{jk} is the coefficient of correlation between the jth project and the kth project. From elementary statistics:

$$M = \sum_{j=1}^{m} \mu_j \qquad (7.4)$$

$$S^2 = \sum_{j=1}^{m} \sigma_j^2 + 2 \sum_{j>k} \rho_{jk}\sigma_j\sigma_k \qquad (7.5)$$

where M and S are the mean and standard deviation of the portfolio.

Any application of Equations (7.4) and (7.5) requires a knowledge of the means and standard deviations of, and the coefficients of correlation between, the NPVs of all projects — both existing and proposed. This is likely to be impractical in most situations. With just ten projects, forty-five different coefficients of correlation would have to be estimated.

Simulation approaches to determining the distribution of NPV for a portfolio of investment projects are described in Cohen and Elton (1967) and Salazar and Sen (1968). These authors suggest that a model relating the net cash flows to other factors should be built for each project in the usual way and that all the projects under consideration should then be simulated jointly. In this model some of the factors to which cash flows are related will be the same for all projects. Dependencies between factors have to be evaluated in the usual way but the overall effect should be that true sources of uncertainty affecting the portfolio as a whole (e.g. GNP, level of competitive activity, etc.) are to some extent considered explicitly.

7.5. The Capital Asset Pricing Model

We now move on to consider the risk in an investment from the point of view of one of the company's shareholders. If it is accepted that a business is operated solely for the benefit of its shareholders then it is important that their interests are considered when a decision on an investment is taken. A shareholder has, in practice, far more diversification opportunities open to him than the company has. He can choose any of the securities which are traded on the Stock Exchange when making up his portfolio. For this reason it is possible for an investment project to have a high marginal risk to the company but a low marginal risk to the shareholder.

The Capital Asset Pricing Model is the key to understanding the nature of the diversification opportunities open to a shareholder. There is now a great deal of empirical evidence in support of the model. Basically, the model divides the risk in an individual security into two parts. The first part — known as the systematic risk — is that part of the total risk which arises from a correlation between the returns from the individual security and the returns from the securities market as a whole. It cannot be diversified away. The second part — known as the unsystematic risk — is unique to the particular security and can be diversified away.

Let R_j be the return from security j during a particular period. R_j is the sum of dividends received and capital gains. For example, if

Price of security at beginning of period= 100
Price of security at end of period   = 112
Dividends received during period   =   5

$$R_j = \frac{(112 - 100) + 5}{100} = 0.17.$$

Let R_m be the return from the securities market as a whole (calculated in a similar way to the Financial Times Actuaries Index). There is a best fit linear relationship between R_j and R_m of the following form:

$$R_j = \alpha_j + \beta_j R_m + u_j \qquad (7.6)$$

where α_j and β_j are constants and u_j is the residual. This relationship is illustrated in Fig. XX. Although R_m does not completely determine R_j, when R_m changes by a certain amount there is a tendency for R_j to change by β_j times that amount. If $\beta_j = 0.5$, the security is half as volatile as the market; if $\beta_j = 2$ the security is twice as volatile as the market, etc.

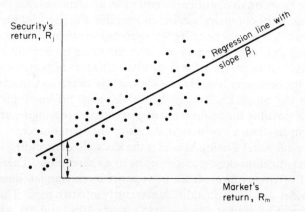

Fig. XX. Relationship between return from an individual security and the return from the market

β_j is a measure of the extent to which the individual security moves with the market. In other words, it is a measure of the security's systematic risk.

The capital asset pricing model shows that it is only a security's systematic risk which is of interest to a well-diversified shareholder. The value of β_j is, therefore, of key importance to the shareholder.

The higher the systematic risk of a security, the higher the return required by the shareholders. The major conclusion of the capital asset pricing model is that the price of security j will adjust so that its expected return $E(R_j)$ is given by

$$E(R_j) = R_f + \beta_j (R_m - R_f) \tag{7.7}$$

where R_f is the risk-free rate of interest. The expected return depends linearly on β_j. When $\beta_j = 0$ the expected return is the risk-free rate. When $\beta_j = 1$ the expected return is the same as that for the market. The relationship in Equation (7.7) is represented graphically in Fig. XXI. The line on Fig. XXI representing the relationship between $E(R_j)$ and β_j is sometimes known as the Capital Market Line.

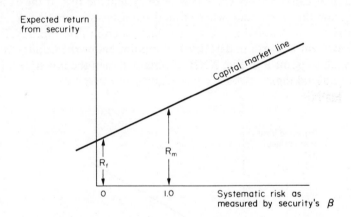

FIG. XXI. Relationship between expected return from a security and its systematic risk

7.6.   Capital Investment and the Shareholder

We are now in a position to consider how a capital investment proposal will be viewed by one of the investing company's shareholders. We have seen that the shareholder is only interested in a security's systematic risk.

For the same reason, he is only interested in the investment proposal's systematic risk, i.e. that part of the risk in the investment proposal which arises from a correlation between the returns from the investment proposal and the returns from the market. The unsystematic risk in an investment proposal can be diversified away by the shareholder using other securities.

The shareholder will, therefore, be interested in defining a "β" for the investment proposal, say β_I, using the best fit linear relationship:

$$R_I = \alpha_I + \beta_I R_m + u_I$$

where R_I is the return from the investment (defined in a similar way to that from a security), u_I is the residual and α_I is a constant.

In deciding whether the investment is worth undertaking, the share holder will be interested in examining whether the expected return from the investment is sufficient to compensate him for the investment's systematic risk. The Capital Market Line in Fig. XXI shows how the return which the shareholder can normally get is related to systematic risk. If the expected return from the investment, when plotted against its systematic risk, gives a return above the Capital Market Line, such as point A in Fig. XXII, then the investment is worth undertaking. If a point below the Capital Market Line, such as point B in Fig. XXII, is obtained then the investment is not worth undertaking.

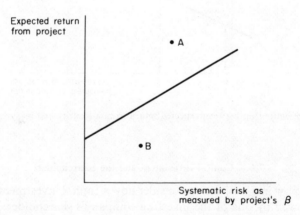

FIG. XXII. Acceptable and non-acceptable projects in relation to the capital market line

One interesting implication of the capital asset pricing model is that diversification by a company in the way described in Section 7.4 is not necessarily in the interests of the shareholders. The company cannot do anything for the shareholders which they are unable to do for themselves. Indeed it can be argued that shareholders would prefer a situation where there were many single industry high risk companies!

The shareholder is, essentially, interested in the company improving its value by finding projects corresponding to points above the Capital Market Line. In a world of perfect competition it is important to note that the company can only expect to find such projects in areas where it enjoys some competitive advantage. The advantage may arise from patents, management-labour relations, customer loyalty, a better location, etc. If no such advantage exists, market forces will tend to reduce the excess return above the Capital Market Line to zero.

It is perhaps worth stressing that using the capital asset pricing model in risk evaluation does assume that the company's sole objective is to maximise shareholders' wealth.

Also, the capital asset pricing model itself involves a number of critical assumptions. It assumes that the market in securities is perfect, with information being freely available to all market participants. It assumes no transaction costs for trading in securities and that the borrowing rate for all market participants is equal to the lending rate. Furthermore, it assumes that, in the event of bankruptcy, all the assets of a company can be sold at their economic value with no selling or legal costs. If some of these assumptions are relaxed then the total risk of a company as well as its systematic risk becomes of importance to the shareholder. It is interesting to note that Van Horne (1977, p. 183) suggests a "dual approach" to investment appraisal where both total risk and systematic risk are evaluated.

7.7 Summary

This chapter has looked at risk and return from the point of view of the individual manager, the company, and the shareholder.

From the point of view of the individual manager who is responsible for an investment decision, it may be the investment's total risk which is important. Furthermore, the individual manager is likely to be using (consciously or unconsciously) a utility function which is more risk averse than that which would be used by the company.

From the point of view of the company, the risk in an investment opportunity can be measured in terms of the marginal contribution which it makes to the company's portfolio of investment projects. The company can generally reduce its overall risk by choosing investment proposals which are not highly correlated with each other.

From the point of view of the shareholder, the risk in an investment opportunity is measured in terms of its marginal contribution to the risk of his portfolio of securities. This in turn is dependent on the correlation between returns from the investment opportunity and returns from the market as a whole.

Which is the correct viewpoint? Theoretically, of course, companies should be acting in the interests of their shareholders. In practice, company managers usually place a high premium on "survival". They find themselves unwilling to take risks which, although small for their well-diversified shareholders, are large for the company.

References

ARROW, K. J. (1965). *Aspects of the theory of risk bearing*, Helsinki: Academic Book Store.
COHEN, K. J. and ELTON, E. J. (1967). Inter-temporal portfolio analysis based on simulation of joint returns, *Management Science*, vol. 14, no. 1, pp. 5–18.
CRAMER, R. H. and SMITH, B. E. (1964). Decision models for the selection of research projects, *Engineering Economist*, vol. 9, pp. 1–20.
GRAYSON, C. J. (1960). *Decisions under uncertainty: drilling decisions by oil and gas operators*, Division of Research, Harvard.
GREEN, P. E. (1963). Risk attitudes and chemical investment decisions, *Chemical Engineering Progress Symposium*, vol. 59, pp. 35–40.
HULL, J. C., MOORE, P. G. and THOMAS, H. (1973). Utility and its measurement, *Journal of Royal Statistical Society*, series A, vol. 136, no. 2, pp. 226–48.
PRATT, J. W. (1964). Risk aversion in the small and in the large, *Econometrica*, vol. 32, pp. 122–36.
SALAZAR, R. C. and SEN, S. K. (1968). A simulation model of capital budgeting under uncertainty, *Management Science*, vol. 15, B, 4, pp. 161–79.
SPETZLER, C. S. (1968). The development of a corporate risk policy for capital investment decisions, *IEE Transactions in Systems Science and Cybernetics*, SSC-4, pp. 279–300.
SWALM, R. O. (1966). Utility theory — insight into risk taking, *Harvard Business Review*, Nov.–Dec., pp. 121–34.
VAN HORNE, J. D. (1977). *Financial management and policy*, 4th edn., Prentice Hall.
VON NEUMANN, J. and MORGENSTERN, O. (1947). *The theory of games and economic behaviour*, Princeton University Press.

Chapter 8
CASE STUDY

8.1. Introduction

This chapter describes a case study illustrating the ideas and techniques which have been discussed in the first seven chapters of the book. The case study is based on a real life investment decision which confronted a major UK chemical company (to be referred to as Crown Chemicals Ltd.) several years ago. The analysis presented is broadly similar to one which was carried out by the company. The reader should bear in mind that, in going from the real life situation to the case study, it has been necessary to make a few changes. For example, in order to preserve confidentiality, the numbers in the case study have had to be altered. Also, to avoid unnecessarily long and involved explanations concerning the environment in which the firm operated, the model has had to be simplified slightly in places. The changes are all relatively minor and do not in any way detract from the value of the case study as a tool for illustrating the methodology of risk evaluation.

8.2. The Model

The investment decision under consideration by Crown Chemicals was whether to build a plant to manufacture a certain industrial chemical product. The product — which we shall refer to as Purinol — had not previously been manufactured in the UK and Crown anticipated that if it went ahead with the project it would be able to capture most of the home market as well as making some sales to its overseas customers. Several different plant sizes were considered. In this chapter we restrict our attention to the way in which the risks associated with a medium-sized plant capable of producing about 200,000 tons of Purinol per annum were evaluated.

115

Once the proposed investment had been clearly defined, the analyst who had been assigned to the project had to identify the different factors liable to affect its performance. Exploratory discussions were held with managers in the three key areas:

> marketing
> production, and
> finance.

The marketing men explained that with a 200,000 tons per annum plant there was a good chance that Crown would be able to sell all that it produced. They considered that the price per ton achieved would depend largely on the vagaries of the market as there was very little scope for Crown adopting a different pricing structure from that of its chief competitors. For various technical reasons the price per ton for sales made to the home market would be £1–£2 higher than for sales made to the export market. In addition, the average cost per ton of delivering Purinol would be higher for overseas customers than for UK customers. The cost of promoting Purinol was expected to be around £100,000 per annum in the home market and £50,000 per annum in the export market. This was because a major sales drive was going to be necessary to develop the home market whereas the existing sales force could, to a large extent, cope with the (somewhat smaller) extra business anticipated overseas.

The initial discussions with production specialists at Crown revealed that the cost of constructing the plant would be between £10M and £11.5M. They were a little concerned about the time which might elapse between the start of construction and the plant becoming fully operational. This, they said, was a factor which was often overlooked by the company; it could be anywhere between 15 and 27 months for a plant capable of producing a substance like Purinol. Certain start-up costs would be incurred during the first year of production. The life of the plant was expected to be between 10 and 15 years and the anticipated salvage value was small (around 5% of capital costs). The fixed cost associated with running and maintaining the plant was expected to be about £1M per year and the production cost per ton was forecast to be in the region of £2.20.

The ·finance department suggested that the proposed analysis should assume a tax rate of 52%. For tax purposes the cost of the investment in the new plant could be written off immediately against profits made elsewhere in the company (and it was expected that such profits would exist). No inflation should be built into the analysis; instead a real "net of inflation" discount rate of 10% per annum should be used. The department stressed the importance of taking into account the investment in working capital as well as that in fixed assets. It was estimated that the former would be around £0.5M.

As will be evident from the discussions in Chapters 1 and 2, the treatment of inflation and the choice of a discount rate recommended by the Finance Department involves a number of crucial assumptions. The evaluation team chose not to challenge these assumptions and decided to produce an analysis where the criteria would correspond as far as possible to existing evaluation procedures within the company.

As a result of his initial discussions, the analyst was able to compile a list of the variables liable to affect the profitability of the investment. This list contained a total of seventeen uncertain variables. These were:

The fixed selling and distribution costs in home market (£ p.a.).
The variable selling and distribution costs in home market (£ per ton).
The price per ton in home market (£).
The potential sales in the home market (tons p.a.).
The fixed selling and distribution costs in the export market (£ p.a.).
The variable selling and distribution costs in the export market (£ per ton).
The price per ton in export market (£).
The potential sales in the export market (tons p.a.).
The capital costs (£).
The date of start up (i.e. years from start of construction).
The life of the plant (years from start up).
The start-up costs (£).
The salvage value (per cent of capital costs).
The fixed costs of production (£ p.a.).
The variable costs of production (£ per ton).
The working capital required (£).
The production capacity (tons).

This list could have been longer. For example, several different home and export markets could have been distinguished, the variable costs of production could have been split into several different categories, etc.

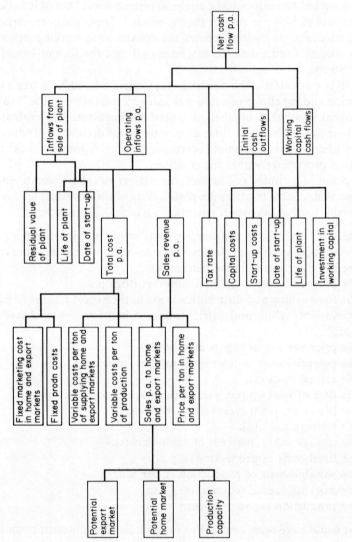

FIG. XXIII. Schematic Representation of the Model

However, for the reasons discussed in Chapter 4, the analyst decided that a highly disaggregated model would create more problems than it would solve. He considered that there would be some advantages in cutting down the number of variables from seventeen to thirteen by dispensing with the distinction between the home market and the export market. However, as the two markets were managed as autonomous entities within the organisation there were compelling arguments against this.

The model which was constructed relating the annual net cash flows to the above variables is shown schematically in Fig. XXIII. It incorporated the following assumptions:

(i) Capital costs occur evenly during the period between the start of construction of the plant and the start of production.

(ii) Start-up costs are incurred as soon as production begins.

(iii) Tax on profits made in one year is paid in the next year, but no other delays occur in the receipt of revenues or the payment of costs.

(iv) The salvage value is realised at the end of the life of the project (i.e. at the time which is given by adding the date of start up to the life of the plant).

(v) The potential sales in the home market, the potential sales in the export market and the production capacity remain constant during the life of the project.

(vi) If the output from the plant is insufficient to satisfy both the home market and the export market then the home market (which is incidentally more profitable) is given priority.

(vii) Working capital requirements remain constant during the life of the plant. Thus a single investment in working capital is made at the start of production and this is recovered at the end of the project.

(viii) There is no tax relief for working capital.

(ix) The fixed costs per annum, the variable costs per ton and the prices per ton for different markets remain constant during the life of the plant.

One final point should be made in connection with the model. The net cash flows which were required for the analysis were *incremental* cash flows; that is, they were the extra cash inflows or outflows which were

TABLE 25. RESULTS OF SENSITIVITY ANALYSIS

Variable	Most likely estimate	Optimistic estimate	Pessimistic estimate	NPV at optimistic estimate £'000s	NPV at pessimistic estimate £'000s	Sensitivity coefficient	Square of sensitivity coefficient	Range coefficient
Life of plant (years)	12	15	10	1278	165	1113	1,238,769	1.00
Capital costs (£'000s)	10,750	10,000	11,500	1050	300	750	562,500	0.67
Production capacity ('000 tons)	200	205	190	891	151	740	547,600	0.66
Price (home market) £ per ton	18.5	19.0	18.0	1024	326	698	487,204	0.63
Fixed production costs (£'000 p.a.)	1000	900	1050	1024	500	524	274,576	0.47
Potential sales (home market) '000s tons	200	210	150	675	221	454	206,116	0.41
Start year	1.75	1.25	2.2	872	522	350	122,500	0.31
Variable costs (home market) £ per ton	1.3	1.1	1.6	814	465	349	121,801	0.31
Variable costs (production) £ per ton	2.20	2.15	2.25	710	640	70	4900	0.06
Fixed costs (home market) £'000s p.a.	100	90	110	710	640	70	4900	0.06
Working capital (£'000s)	500	450	550	707	642	65	4225	0.06
Fixed costs (export market) £'000s p.a.	50	45	55	692	657	35	1225	0.03
Start costs (£'000s)	180	160	200	690	660	30	900	0.03
Salvage value (%)	5	6	4	684	665	19	361	0.02
Potential sales (export market) '000s tons	50	100	30	675	675	:	:	0.00
Variable costs (export market) £ per ton	2.4	2.9	2.0	675	675	:	:	0.00
Price (export market) £ per ton	17.0	17.5	16.5	675	675	:	:	0.00

expected to arise as a result of the investment being undertaken. This had implications for the way in which the individual variables were defined. For example, the fixed costs per annum associated with the export market were defined as the extra costs which would be incurred by the company in that market if the company went ahead with the project. This is quite different from defining them as the costs which, for accounting purposes, would be allocated to Purinol if the company went ahead with the project.

8.3. The Initial Analyses

The first step in the analysis involved asking management to make "pessimistic", "optimistic" and "most likely" estimates for each of the seventeen variables listed in the previous section. Once the importance of evaluating risk had been explained, most managers were fairly willing to co-operate. As explained in Chapter 3, the main danger at this stage is that a manager's attention is initially concentrated on the "most likely value" or "best guess" to such an extent that the optimistic and pessimistic estimates do not reflect the full range of uncertainty. Accordingly, the analyst made every effort to direct managerial attention initially towards extreme scenarios. The pessimistic estimate was defined as that value of the variable which had a 95% chance of being bettered and the optimistic estimate was defined as that value of the variable which had only a 5% chance of being bettered.

The estimates which were made and the results which were obtained from the initial sensitivity analysis are shown in Table 25. The value of NPV (in £'000s) shows that changing a single variable from its best estimate to its pessimistic estimate does not cause NPV to be negative. However, it seems likely from the magnitude of the numbers in the table that changes in two or more variables could make NPV negative.

It will be recalled from Chapter 5 that the sensitivity coefficient of a variable is the difference between the value of the performance measure when the variable is put equal to its optimistic estimate and the value of the performance measure when the variable is put equal to its pessimistic estimate, all other variables being kept fixed at their best estimates. (The range coefficient of a variable is defined here as the ratio of its sensitivity coefficient to the sensitivity coefficient of the most sensitive variable.) Various ways in which the sensitivity coefficient can be interpreted were discussed in Chapter 5. It was pointed out that if S_i is the sensitivity coefficient of the ith variable then a very crude approximation to the standard deviation of the performance measure is:

$$0.3 \sqrt{\sum_i S_i^2} \qquad (8.1)$$

when the pessimistic and optimistic estimates correspond to 5 and 95 percentiles. Furthermore the proportion of the total variance of NPV accounted for by variable j is approximately:

$$\frac{S_j^2}{\sum S_i^2} \qquad (8.2)$$

In this case, $\sum S_i^2$ is (from the penultimate column in Table 21) 3,577,577 indicating that the standard deviation of NPV (£'000s) is in the region of 500 to 600. It follows from this that the mean and standard deviation of NPV are approximately equal and that some further evaluation of the investment's risk is likely to be valuable.

Equation (8.2) and the penultimate column of Table 25 suggest that:

(a) the eight most sensitive variables can be expected to account for over 99% of the variance of NPV; and

(b) the four most sensitive variables can be expected to account for about 80% of the variance of NPV.

However, Table 25 is slightly misleading in that it gives the impression that NPV is totally insensitive to three of the variables: the potential sales in the export market, the price in the export market and the variable costs in the export market. This is because, when each variable is put equal to its best estimate, there is no surplus production once the home market has been supplied. As a check on the possible importance of the above three variables a further sensitivity analysis was carried out based on the assumption that the size of the home market was equal to its pessimistic estimate (i.e. 150,000 tons). The results are summarised in Table 26. It is clear from this table that Table 25 underestimates the importance of all three variables. The variable potential sales (export markets) becomes particularly important as soon as the size of the home market drops below its best estimate.

A similar argument can be used to show that Table 25 underestimates the importance of the variable potential sales (home market). In fact, when the

TABLE 26. SENSITIVITY ANALYSIS ASSUMING
THAT THE HOME MARKET IS ONLY 150,000 TONS

Variable	Sensitivity coefficient
Potential sales (export market) '000 tons	865
Price (export market) £ per ton	174
Variable costs (export market) £ per ton	157

size of the export market is put equal to its pessimistic estimate (i.e. 30,000 tons), the sensitivity coefficient of this variable becomes 1139 (instead of 454).

On the basis of the above analyses it is clear that the only variables which are liable to be important are the top eight variables in Table 25 plus the variable potential sales (export market). Table 27 classifies these variables as "sensitive" and the remainder as "non-sensitive".

TABLE 27. CLASSIFICATION OF VARIABLES

Sensitive	Non-sensitive
Life of plant	Variable costs (production)
Capital costs	Fixed costs (home market)
Production capacity	Working capital
Price (home market)	Fixed costs (export market)
Potential sales (home market)	Start costs
Fixed production costs	Salvage value
Start year	Variable costs (export market)
Variable costs (home market)	Price (export market)
Potential sales (export market)	

8.4. The First Simulations

In the first exploratory simulation the variables classified as "non-sensitive" (see Table 27) were described by a point estimate and those classified as "sensitive" were approximated to by a triangular distribution (see Fig. X).

The point estimate which was chosen for a non-sensitive variable was equal to the PERT estimate of the variable's mean, i.e. it was

$$\frac{1}{6} (U + 4M + L)$$

where U, M and L are the optimistic, most likely and pessimistic estimate of the variable. The parameters of the triangular distribution were chosen so that the mean of the triangular distribution was

$$\frac{1}{6} (U + 4M + L)$$

and the standard deviation was

$$0.3 \ (U - L).$$

A discussion of the rationale behind all this and a description of the way in which the parameters of the triangular distribution can be calculated is given in Section 5.9.

The distribution of NPV which was obtained is shown in Fig. XXIV. The distribution is based on 1000 runs. It is approximately normal with a mean of 534 and a standard deviation of 580. To a large extent the distribution confirms the initial "quick and dirty" analyses described in Section 8.3.

Throughout this study management expressed particular interest in

Percentage probability (NPV > 0)

This statistic will be referred to as the "critical percentage". Fig. XXIV indicates that it is 84%.

In addition to producing Fig. XXIV the first run of the simulation investigated the potential effect of dependencies between the variables categorised as sensitive in Table 27. Discussions with management had revealed four such dependencies:

(a) Potential sales in export market positively dependent on potential sales in home market.
(b) Potential sales in home market positively dependent on price in home market.
(c) Fixed production costs positively dependent on production capacity.
(d) Start year positively dependent on capital costs.

The simulation tested the effect on the distribution of NPV of assuming perfect dependence in each of the above four cases. (Chapter 4 provides a

```
   LESS THAN        -1700.00    I
-1700.00    TO      -1600.00    I
-1600.00    TO      -1500.00    IX
-1500.00    TO      -1400.00    IX
-1400.00    TO      -1300.00    IX
-1300.00    TO      -1200.00    I
-1200.00    TO      -1100.00    I
-1100.00    TO      -1000.00    IXX
-1000.00    TO       -900.00    IXX
 -900.00    TO       -800.00    IXX
 -800.00    TO       -700.00    IXXX
 -700.00    TO       -600.00    IYYXY
 -600.00    TO       -500.00    IXXXYXXX
 -500.00    TO       -400.00    IXXXXXXXXX
 -400.00    TO       -300.00    IXXXXXXXX
 -300.00    TO       -200.00    IYXXXXXXXXXXXXX
 -200.00    TO       -100.00    IXXXXXXXXYXXXYX
 -100.00    TO          0.00    IXXXXXXXXXYYXXXXXXXXXXX
    0.00    TO        100.00    IXXXXXXXXXXYXXXXXXXXXXXXXX
  100.00    TO        200.00    IYYYXXXXYXYXYXXXXYXXXXXXXXXXXXXXXXXXXXY
  200.00    TO        300.00    IXXXXYXXXXXXXYXXXYXXXYXXXYYYYY
  300.00    TO        400.00    IXXXXXXXXYYXYXXXYYXXXXXXXXYXXX
  400.00    TO        500.00    IXXXXXXXYYYXXYXXXXXXXXXXXYYXXXXXXXXXXXXYYXY
  500.00    TO        600.00    IXXXYXXXXYYYXYXXXYYXXXXXXXXXXXXXX
  600.00    TO        700.00    IXXXXXXXYXXXXXXXXYXXXXXXXXXXXXXXXXXX
  700.00    TO        800.00    IXXXXXXXXYXXXXXXXXXXXXXXXXXXXX
  800.00    TO        900.00    IYXXXXXXXYXXXYXXXYXXXXXXXXXXXXYY
  900.00    TO       1000.00    IXXXXXXXXYXXXXXXXXXXXXXXXX
 1000.00    TO       1100.00    IXXXXXXXXYXYXYXXXXXXXXYXXXXY
 1100.00    TO       1200.00    IXXXXXXXYXXYXXXXXXXXX
 1200.00    TO       1300.00    IYXYYXXXYXXXXXXXXXXX
 1300.00    TO       1400.00    IXXXXXXXYXXXXXXXXX
 1400.00    TO       1500.00    IXYXXXXXXXXX
 1500.00    TO       1600.00    IXYXYYX
 1600.00    TO       1700.00    IXXXY
 1700.00    TO       1800.00    IYXX
 1800.00    TO       1900.00    IXYYX
 1900.00    TO       2000.00    IX
 2000.00    TO       2100.00    IXY
 2100.00    TO       2200.00    IX
 2200.00    TO       2300.00    IXX
 2300.00    TO       2400.00    I
 2400.00    TO       2500.00    I
 2500.00    TO       2600.00    I
 2600.00    TO       2700.00    I
 2700.00    TO       2800.00    I
GREATER THAN         2900.00    I
```

FIG. XXIV. Initial distribution of NPV (£'000s)

discussion of the meaning of the term "perfect dependence" in this context.) The results are summarised in Table 28. None of the dependencies are likely to have a great effect on the distribution of NPV. The most important one is the first one. This on its own could reduce the critical percentage to about 80%.

TABLE 28. EFFECT OF DEPENDENCIES ON DISTRIBUTION OF NPV

Dependent variable	Independent variable	Change in mean of NPV if total dependence	Change in standard deviation of NPV if total dependence	Change in critical percentage if total dependence
Potential sales (export market)	Potential sales (home market)	−71	+100	−4.4
Potential sales (home market)	Price (home market)	+21	+ 17	−1.4
Fixed costs (production)	Production capacity	+ 6	− 43	+2.2
Start year	Capital costs	+14	+ 49	−1.8

The formulae derived in Sections 5.3 and 5.7 were then used to estimate for the seven most sensitive variables in Table 25.

(a) The effect on the mean of NPV of increasing the mean of the variable by 5% of its range.

(b) The effect on the standard deviation of NPV of increasing the standard deviation of the variable by 30%.

The results are shown in Table 29.

TABLE 29. ESTIMATE OF EFFECT OF ERRORS IN MEANS AND STANDARD DEVIATIONS OF VARIABLES

Variable	Effect on mean of NPV of change in mean of variable equal to 5% of range	Effect on standard deviation of 30% change in standard deviation of variable
Life of plant	56	58
Capital costs	38	26
Production capacity	37	25
Price (home market)	35	23
Fixed production costs	26	13
Potential sales (home market)	23	10
Start year	17	6
Var cost (home market)	17	6

8.5.   Further Analyses

At this stage, the analyst wrote a report which included the distribution shown in Fig. XXIII and a brief explanation of how it had been obtained. A meeting of all top management involved in the proposed project was then arranged so that

(i)   the analyst could initiate a discussion of the model, its assumptions and the output so far;

(ii) an "acceptable level of risk" could be established;

(iii) a future course of action could be agreed upon.

The importance of "progress meetings" such as this cannot be emphasised too much. They ensure first that top management are aware of what the analyst is doing and, second, that the work of the analyst is actually relevant to the problem under consideration. In any model building exercise the biggest danger is that the analyst will lose touch with reality to such an extent that he provides a perfectly accurate answer to the wrong problem. To quote Carter (1972): "although many management scientists are reluctant to acknowledge the fact, it is often true that their exact solution to the approximate problem is not as good as the approximate solution to the exact problem".

In this particular instance there was relatively little disagreement about the validity of the model which had been used. This was probably because the model was similar to others which had been used (on a deterministic basis) by the same company for previous investments in chemical plants.

The portfolio considerations described in the previous chapter were discussed at this stage. It was decided that the project was fairly closely correlated with the performance of the company as a whole and that few risk diversification benefits could be expected. The fact that the shareholder might be able to diversify away some of the risk was not considered and the company agreed that the prime consideration was the project's total risk.

The question of what was an acceptable level of risk for the project provoked a great deal of discussion. As has already been mentioned, management were most concerned with the critical percentage:

Percentage probability (NPV > 0)

This percentage is 84 for the distribution in Fig. XXIII and it was eventually agreed that this was acceptable. It is, however, worth noting that for any company or group of managers the acceptability of a critical percentage can be expected to depend on the size of the project (the bigger the project, the higher the critical percentage must be).

The analyst explained that the distribution in Fig. XXIII was not perfect because relatively few estimates had been made for the different variables. He asked how far the critical percentage could fall before the project became unacceptable. This was a difficult question to answer but eventually a figure of 75 was agreed upon as the "breakeven critical percentage".

It was finally agreed that further assessments and analyses should be carried out as the analyst considered necessary, and another meeting was arranged for a fortnight later.

The question which the analyst then had to consider was: to what extent is it possible that further assessments could reduce the critical percentage to below 75? Assuming that the distribution of NPV remains approximately normal, it is easy to show that, for a critical percentage of less than 75:

$$\mu_{NPV} < 0.67\ \sigma_{NPV}$$

where μ_{NPV} and σ_{NPV} are the mean and standard deviation of NPV. From Tables 28 and 29 it seems unlikely that further assessments on any one variable could reduce the critical percentage from 84 to 75. It is just possible that further assessments on several variables could do so (particularly if it is accepted that thinking more deeply about a variable can actually cause a manager to change his mind about his initial assessments!).

The analyst decided, in the event, to quantify the distributions of

> life of plant
> capital costs
> production capacity
> price (home market)
> potential sales (home market)

more precisely and to evaluate the extent of the dependence between the potential sales in the home market and the potential sales in the export market. The probability distributions were obtained using fixed interval methods in the way described in Chapter 3. The quantification of the dependence between potential sales in the home market and potential sales in the export market involved the model of dependence described in Appendix C with several judgements of the form: If home market potential sales = 175,000, median estimate for export market potential sales = 40,000.

The distribution of NPV which was output from a further simulation incorporating all the assessments was approximately normal with a mean of 630, a standard deviation of 650 and a critical percentage of 85. This was encouraging news for the next meeting. It was considered highly unlikely that any further precision in the estimates could reduce the critical percentage to below 75 and the project was eventually accepted.

8.6.   Summary and Conclusions

The approach used in this case study is illustrated in Fig. XXV. It is indicative of the sort of approach which can be used in virtually any situation where an evaluation of an investment's risk is required.

The approach is designed with two key observations about risk simulation in mind:

(i) A major reason why risk simulation has not been widely accepted is the large number of probability assessments which management are typically required to make for a risk simulation (see Longbottom and Wade, 1971, and Carter, 1972).

(ii) The cost of the computer time used to carry out a risk simulation once the cash flow model has been developed is, at the present time, trivial (see Bonini, 1975).

The essence of the approach is that assessments are only made at one stage of the analysis if they have been indicated as being necessary at a previous stage. One significant advantage of the approach is that very often no detailed probability assessments are required from management at all because the decision is clear cut at an early stage. If detailed probability assessments are required then the approach will keep these to a minimum and it will put the analyst in a position where he is able to explain the importance of the assessments to management.

The number of different test risk simulations carried out is not as

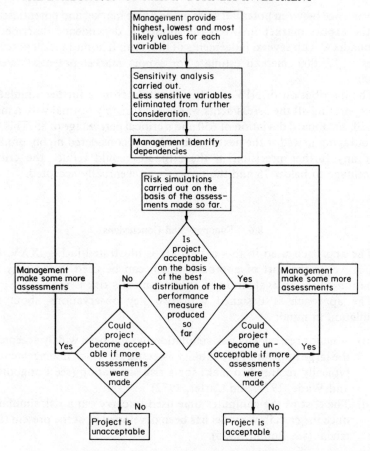

FIG. XXV. Procedure for evaluation of investment risk

wasteful of computer time as it might appear. In the analyses described in this chapter, 1000 simulations runs were used to provide the main distributions and 500 were used when a comparison between two different distributions was required (e.g. for Table 29). The total computer time for all analyses was less than 7 minutes.

References

BONINI, C. P. (1975). Risk evaluation of investment projects, *OMEGA*, vol. 3, no. 5, pp. 735–50.
CARTER, E. E. (1972). What are the risks in risk analysis, *Harvard Business Review*, July–Aug., pp. 72–82.
LONGBOTTOM, D. A. and WADE, G. (1971). *The application of decision analysis in United Kingdom Companies*, Durham University Business School Research Paper No. 1.

Chapter 9
INTRODUCING RISK EVALUATION
INTO AN ORGANISATION

9.1. Introduction

What is it that determines the success or failure of risk evaluation within an organisation? One is tempted, after reading the first eight chapters of this book, to answer that the specialists who are recruited to carry out the analyses are all important. They must be competent enough to build models which include the right variables, to elicit meaningful probability judgements from management, to deal with dependences between variables in a sensible way . . . and so on. However, the successful implementation of risk evaluation depends on far more than just technical competence. Ultimately, the success or failure of risk evaluation (or of any other innovation in business) is determined by a whole battery of organisational and behavioural forces. In this chapter we shall explore the nature of these forces and draw some conclusions about how a company should introduce risk evaluation in order to maximise its chances of success.

There have been a number of surveys carried out and articles written concerned with the implementation of risk evaluation and other management science techniques in business. All have emphasised the importance of organisational and behavioural factors. To quote from the final paragraph of Wagner's well-known textbook on Operational Research (see Wagner, 1969):

"The time is past when an operations researcher can build a mathematical model and remain impervious to the behavioural characteristics of the individuals affected and the organisational milieu. Visionaries among operations research professionals are fully aware that new developments such as those described above exert

132

tremendous strains on the managerial fabric of a corporate organisation. To enhance the adoption of these technical and technological advances by industry and government, management and behavioural scientists together will have to find ways by which executives can deal effectively with computerised systems as beneficial change agents."

Most managers naturally resist changes — particularly those changes which involve complicated mathematical models that they do not fully understand and do not have fully under their control. Most management scientists, on the other hand, enjoy model building for its own sake and are not particularly interested in the behavioural problems associated with the implementation of their models. Clearly, there is plenty of scope for conflicts and misunderstandings in this situation and, unless management scientists as a group are carefully integrated into an organisation, the chances are that their impact on that organisation will be negligible.

Perhaps the most interesting study of the implementation of risk evaluation in business has been carried out by Carter (1972). He interviewed executives in four major oil companies that had decided to try risk evaluation and came to the conclusion that the success of the technique depended on answers to a number of questions such as:

> What was the impetus to introduce risk evaluation?
> Where was the management science department located?
> How well educated were the users?
> What was top management's role?
> Who was assigned to shepherd the project?

This chapter will *inter alia* examine Carter's findings in some detail.

9.2. Some General Observations

Before any steps are taken to introduce risk evaluation into an organisation, some thought needs to be given to the question of whether the organisation is "ready" for the technique. How does it appraise capital investment projects at present? Does it use NPV or IRR? Does it carry out a sensitivity analysis?

To take an extreme situation, if a company does not at present make detailed cash-flow forecasts as part of its procedure for assessing major capital investment projects, then it is highly unlikely that it will suddenly be able to start coping successfully with a probability distribution for NPV. The analyst, before he does anything else, must become thoroughly familiar with existing procedures. He should determine not only what the formal written down procedures are, but also how these procedures are used in practice.

The development of a capital budgeting system should be regarded as a matter of evolution, not revolution. As far as the evaluation of risk is concerned, companies can often be seen to evolve in five stages:

Stage 1. No account is taken of risk. If IRRs or NPVs are calculated, the same rate of return is required for all projects.

Stage 2. Project risk is assessed subjectively as high, medium or low. The higher the risk, the higher the required rate of return.

Stage 3. A sensitivity analysis is carried out by making a fixed percentage change to each variable for all projects above a certain size.

Stage 4. For all projects above a certain size, optimistic, most likely, and pessimistic estimates are made for each variable, and a sensitivity analysis based on the estimates is carried out.

Stage 5. The company makes some use of risk simulation for large projects.

The analyst should carefully evaluate which stage his company is at and whether it would benefit from moving on to the next stage. Possibly one of the biggest reasons for the failure of management science models in business is the management scientist's tendency to want to make his model as "sophisticated" and as "realistic" as possible without taking due account of how it will fit into his company's decision-making processes at their current stage of evolution.

9.3. Gaining Acceptance for Risk Evaluation

The philosophy of analysing risks is not one which has achieved complete acceptance by either the business or the academic communities. Hall (1975), for example, in a provocative article entitled "Why risk analysis isn't working" advocates that managers should be encouraged to find ways of living with risks rather than analysing them. He considers that "the oft-maligned philosophy of taking them as they come will rise again". How can one gain acceptance in industry for some form of risk evaluation? One of the problems here (and this is not a problem which is shared by all other management science techniques) is that it is difficult — perhaps impossible — to prove that the technique will lead to better decisions or improved profits. Even if we know in a certain situation that the output of a risk evaluation study influenced a manager to take decision A rather than decision B, we will not know for several years how decision A turns out and even then we may not be sure about what would have happened if decision B had been taken. Furthermore, suppose that it is definitely established that decision A turned out *worse* than decision B would have done, an advocate of risk evaluation will, undaunted, argue along the following lines:

"It was a good decision — just an unlucky outcome. We were in the extreme left-hand tail of the distribution of NPV's."

And this is the heart of the problem. There are never likely to be enough major capital investment decisions facing a company within a reasonable period of time for it to be proved statistically that decisions taken on the basis of an analysis of the risks are better than those taken without any such analysis.

It should be recognised that the use of risk evaluation in business is in essence an "act of faith". Proponents of risk evaluation believe that the more quantitative information an executive has about the risks inherent in an investment opportunity, and the more he understands the nature of the risks, the better his decisions concerning that investment opportunity will be.

This raises questions as to whose "act of faith" is important. Certainly the management science professionals within the organisation which is introducing risk evaluation must believe in the technique. Also, the technique is not likely to get very far if divisional managers and others with capital budgeting responsibilities are opposed to any kind of formal risk evaluation. As with all innovations in business, it is the extent of top management support — and the quality of that support — which is likely to be crucial to success. Top management must ensure that risk evaluation is incorporated in a sensible and effective way into the capital budgeting procedures. They must themselves understand the *modus operandi* of risk evaluation and they must be prepared to step in and sort out disputes between management scientists and the middle managers who are the users of the technique. Typically, the middle managers are initially strongly in favour of risk evaluation — but this enthusiasm wains when they realise that they themselves must spend a not inconsiderable amount of time discussing investment opportunities with the management scientists and providing estimates for the variables in the risk evaluation models. Unless top management support is very evident during the early stages of the introduction of risk evaluation, it is not likely to be given a fair test.

This leads on to another prime requirement for the successful introduction of risk evaluation. Those middle managers whose work will be most affected by the use of the technique must be involved in its introduction from the outset. A working party consisting of representatives from all the involved departments should be set up as early as possible. It should discuss at what stage in the capital budgeting process inputs to the risk evaluation model will be provided, who will provide those inputs, what form the outputs will take, and so on. Changes can rarely be introduced into an organisation by presenting managers with a *fait accompli*. Only if a manager feels that he has participated in the decision to make a change will he feel committed to making it work. Otherwise, he is liable to feel threatened by the change and may even decide to devote his energies to making sure that it does *not* work.

Another key element in the successful introduction of risk evaluation is education. It is a natural human tendency to resent and rebel against that which is not understood. Prior to the introduction of risk evaluation, a company should embark on an educational programme designed to explain to middle and senior managers exactly what the technique is trying to achieve and how it works. The mystique which sometimes surrounds a computer application such as risk evaluation should, as far as possible, be removed. Managers should fully appreciate the importance of quantifying their uncertainties about different variables and should be quite clear about the difference between:

(i) The uncertainty in NPV which is due to management's uncertainty about the value of a single variable.
(ii) The uncertainty in NPV which is due to management's uncertainty about the values of all variables.

The precise way in which (ii) is calculated may not be completely understood, but managers should gain some qualitative feel for the way in which uncertainties combine together when variables are (a) added together and (b) multiplied together. Often it is useful to take a project which the company has recently evaluated and to show how risk evaluation would have assisted top management in reaching a decision.

9.4. The Costs and Benefits of Risk Evaluation

This book has stressed the benefits which can be obtained from a carefully carried out sensitivity analysis based on optimistic and pessimistic estimates for the variables. Very often a full-risk simulation will not be required or will not be thought worthwhile. From top management's point of view the costs of incorporating risk evaluation into its capital budgeting procedures will usually consist of:

(a) the cost of the time of middle and senior managers in discussing and defining investment opportunities with management scientists;

(b) the cost of the time of middle and senior managers in providing best, optimistic and pessimistic estimates for variables;

(c) the cost of the time of the management scientists and computer programmers;

(d) the cost of the computer time used.

All of these are, strictly speaking, opportunity costs and as such they may be difficult to determine. For example, in order to work out the cost of the time of managers and management scientists, in theory we need to know how they would spend the time that would be released by the abandonment of risk evaluation. This is clearly no easy matter! The cost of computer time might be thought more straightforward — but even here there can be complications. Suppose that a company plans to use its own computer which is not currently operating at capacity. The opportunity cost of computer time to the company might be calculated as zero. But it must be remembered that most companies are continually embarking on new computer applications. In a few years time the use of risk evaluation in capital budgeting could well lead to the company buying a new computer earlier than it would do otherwise. This would represent a real cost to the company.

What are the benefits of risk evaluation which can be weighed against the costs? We have pointed out that it cannot be proved statistically that risk evaluation improves decision making. However, there are certain concrete advantages of risk evaluation which should be emphasised. Risk evaluation provides a quantitative measure of the risk in an investment opportunity. Different investment opportunities can be ranked according to their riskiness so that the company is then able to make its risk-return trade-offs in a clearer way.

Risk evaluation also has the big advantage that it distinguishes the important uncertainties from the unimportant uncertainties in a particular investment project. Variables which are thought to be of major importance by some managers, and which are the source of managerial disagreements, are often shown to be relatively insignificant. Generally, risk evaluation quickly focuses managerial attention onto the key uncertainties. Sometimes, as has been mentioned in the course of this book, ways are even found whereby these uncertainties can be reduced.

Furthermore, the fact that risk evaluation forces managers to think objectively about the uncertainties in their environment, and to make forecasts in terms of ranges rather than single values, is itself an advantage. To quote Carter (1972):

"... explicit consideration of risk and return does sharpen thinking. Because it makes disagreements between project managers explicit, and because it put the importance of various factors into perspective, perhaps the greatest benefit of risk analysis comes from the preparation of the model, not from the results."

9.5. The Organisation of Risk Evaluation

The way in which risk evaluation is organised within a company has been shown to be critical to its success. Problems arise when the management science activity is highly centralised and projects are generated at the divisional level. The management scientist will then feel no identity with, or loyalty towards, the division he happens to be working with at a particular time. He will be considered an outsider by the division and his presence is likely to be resented. He may well be branded as a "spy from head office". In any event, he is likely to be afforded only minimal co-operation and divisional managers will be reluctant to reveal to him confidential information or sensitive data which might be passed back to head office. Every management scientist must spend enough time on the head office staff to become thoroughly familiar with the full range of management science applications within his company. But many of the problems which are encountered in manager/management scientist relationships will be overcome if virtually every management scientist is attached permanently to a particular division as a staff officer as soon as possible. The first loyalties of the management scientist will then be towards the division. The chances are that he will be trusted by the division's management and that he will, as a result, be far more effective. Not every management scientist is likely to be happy working in a divisional environment. Some management scientists identify strongly with their field and not with their company. They prefer developing new techniques to implementing established ones. Often a company must be prepared to let these people go if it wishes to maintain a successful implementation-oriented management science function. There may be some room for them at head office — but a company should always try to avoid becoming top heavy with theoreticians.

Ideally, risk evaluation should be organised as a "group activity" at the divisional level with divisional finance officers, divisional management scientists and divisional computer experts all working closely together. The aim of the group should be to maximise its influence over the capital budgeting process. Rather than attempting to change the whole nature of that process, it should strive to become an integral part of it. It should ensure that it produces good, well-argued reports in time for the right meetings. There may be some small psychological satisfaction in producing a perfect analysis of a project after a decision on the project has been taken — but such an analysis will have little impact and may even lead to unnecessary hostility towards risk evaluation. A slightly imperfect analysis produced on time is always preferable to a perfect analysis produced late.

Another aspect of the organisation of risk evaluation which deserves some consideration concerns the computer programs. Very often a division will be using standard computer programs developed elsewhere in the company or by an outside agency. These programs should always be capable of being adapted to fit in with the requirements of a particular project. The project's specification should not have to be adapted to fit in with the program. This may seem an obvious point but it is surprising how often an enthusiastic management scientist or computer programmer will attempt to write an "all purpose" computer program using standard variables, a standard model and producing output in a standard invariable format.

In the author's opinion the computer subroutines which are given at the end of this book provide a useful basis from which a company can develop its own suite of programs. The subroutines enable the user to sample from probability distributions, carry out sensitivity analysis, calculate NPVs and IRRs, print out histograms and so on fairly effortlessly. However, the input variables, and the model which is used to calculate cash flows from the input variables must be defined by the user. Generally, these will vary from project to project and standard variables with a standard model are only really likely to be appropriate if a series of projects all identical in structure are being analysed by the same company.

9.6. Obtaining Assessments

There is little doubt that the single most difficult part of risk evaluation is the generation of good input data. The input data for a sensitivity analysis consists of most likely, optimistic, and pessimistic estimates for each of the variables. A risk simulation requires, in addition, that probabilistic estimates be made for the more important variables and that other estimates be provided concerning dependencies between these variables. Although an analysis of historical data can sometimes be helpful in providing these estimates, it is usually necessary to rely heavily on subjective judgements made by experienced managers.

It is an unfortunate fact of life that executives are nearly always reticent when it comes to providing concrete estimates of any sort. They feel that the numbers which they come up with may be "used against them" at some future stage. Risk evaluation which works in terms of ranges rather than single estimates should, in theory, make the whole process less threatening. This is not always the case, as managers are sometimes reluctant to admit the full extent of their uncertainty about certain variables. A marketing executive, for example, might feel that it is part of his job to "know" what the market for a certain product will be and he might consider it important to his career progression that he sound confident and precise when making estimates about it.

How in the light of all these difficulties should the assessment process be handled? Unfortunately, there are no easy answers. Chapter 3 includes a number of suggestions as to how biases can be overcome and managers forced to commit themselves. Possibly the most useful of these suggestions is what might be termed the "extreme scenario" approach where the analyst presents the manager with more and more extreme scenarios. Eventually, while arguing about these, the manager gives his true opinions as to what could happen. It should also be remembered that optimistic and pessimistic estimates should be obtained before best estimates. Otherwise the manager is liable to "anchor onto" the best estimate and produce a range which is far too narrow.

In this book we have stressed the value of a step-by-step approach to risk evaluation where assessments are only made by managers at one stage when they have been shown to be necessary at a previous stage. This approach is, in the author's opinion, the only one which can lead to wholehearted acceptance for risk evaluation within an organisation. Indeed, as has been pointed out earlier in this chapter, one of the key advantages of risk evaluation is that it is capable of focusing managerial attention onto important variables. It would be a pity not to use this advantage to the full. Executives are likely to be far more receptive to an analyst who is asking for estimates when that analyst can actually explain why the estimates are important. To quote again from Carter (1972):

"... my impression is that companies tend to jump the gun on the question of obtaining 'good data'. One of the benefits of risk analysis is that it shows management the relative impact of the uncertainties in different factors — to some extent it ranks the factors in order of importance. Using only crude distributions of uncertainty in various components an analysis can quickly reveal where the company ought to spend more time refining the data, and where the final results would be only minimally changed even with a large magnitude of error in the input data."

The obtaining of assessments must, therefore, be regarded as a sequential process. First the basic three estimates (most likely, optimistic, and pessimistic) are made for each variable. A sensitivity analysis is then carried out. The results are relayed back to management. Further consideration is given to the most sensitive variable with, possibly, some of the initial estimates being revised. Further analyses are carried out. If considered necessary, a few key probabilistic estimates are then made in readiness for a risk simulation.

The provision of feedback to management is absolutely crucial to the success of the above process. Without feedback, making estimates will rapidly become a game or a ritualistic form-filling-in exercise. The feedback should provide a focus for continuing dialogues between the risk evaluation group and senior management. It will sort out misunderstandings at an early stage and possibly lead to important revisions to the basic cash flow model.

9.7. Summary

If risk evaluation is to be successfully introduced into a company, managers and management scientists must work closely together at all stages. The initial impetus for introducing risk evaluation should come from top management. An educational programme should then be set up to explain to the middle and senior managers exactly what the technique is trying to achieve and how it works. A working party with representatives from all involved departments should be formed to discuss how the technique will fit into the company's present capital budgeting procedures, when the input should be provided, what form the output should take, and so on.

In a large company the management science specialists who are involved in risk evaluation will only be fully effective if they are attached on a full-time basis to particular divisions. They should not assume the roles of "consultants from head office". Within the division, risk evaluation should be set up as a team effort — not as something which is solely the responsibility of the management scientist. The team should consist of divisional finance officers, divisional management scientists, and divisional computer experts. They should ensure that they have maximum impact on the capital budgeting review process by producing timely, well-argued reports.

Finally, the obtaining of estimates from management should be regarded as a multi-stage process. Initially, management must provide most likely, optimistic and pessimistic estimates for each variable. At a later stage further estimates — or more precise estimates — may be required by the risk evaluation team. It should by then always be possible for members of the team to explain why the extra information is important and how it will be used.

References

CARTER, E. E. (1972). What are the risks in risk analysis, *Harvard Business Review*, July–Aug., pp. 72–82.
HALL, W. K. (1975). Why risk analysis isn't working, *Long Range Planning*, Dec., pp. 25–9.
WAGNER, H. M. (1969). *Principles of operations research; with applications to managerial decisions*, Prentice-Hall.

Appendix A
A COMPUTER PROGRAM FOR CARRYING OUT SENSITIVITY ANALYSES

A.1. Introduction

The computer program RISKANAL1 described in this Appendix is a series of Fortran subroutines for carrying out a sensitivity analysis of the performance of a capital investment project. The user of the program must provide:

(i) optimistic, pessimistic and best (i.e. most likely) estimates for each variable affecting the performance of the investment. (For a discussion of the definitions of the terms "optimistic estimate", "pessimistic estimate" and "best estimate" see chapter 5); and

(ii) a subroutine for calculating the net cash flows in each year from a given set of values for the variables.

The output from the program shows the effect on the performance measure of putting individual variables equal to their optimistic and pessimistic estimates while keeping all other variables fixed at their best estimates. The program also uses the analysis in Chapter 5 to estimate the mean of the performance measure, the standard deviation of the performance measure, and the percentage of the variance of the performance measure accounted for by each variable.

A.2. The Input

RISKANAL1 can deal with up to fifty variables and carry out the sensitivity analysis for up to five different performance measures. The performance measures can be either NPV with a specified discount rate, or IRR. The desire to use IRR is indicated in the input by the specification of a discount rate of –100% (see card 3 below).

The format of the input is as follows:

Card 1 (cols. 1–24)	A title for the project (up to twenty-four characters).
Card 2 (col. 5)	The number of different performance measures to be considered (must be not more than five).
Card 3 (cols. 1–10)	Percentage discount rate for first performance measure. Decimal point is in column 8; two places of decimals are after decimal point. (IRR is indicated by a percentage discount rate of –100.00).
Card 3 (cols. 11–20, 21–30, 31–40, 41–50)	(As necessary.) Percentage discount rates for second, third, fourth and fifth performance measures. Decimal points are in columns 18, 28, 38 and 48; two places of decimals are after decimal point (IRR is indicated by a percentage discount rate of –100.00).
Card 4 (cols. 4–5, right justified)	The number of different variables (must be not more than fifty).
Card 5 (cols. 1–16)	Name of first variable (up to sixteen characters).
Card 5 (cols. 17–24)	Best estimate for first variable. Decimal point is in column 22; two places of decimals are after decimal point.
Card 5 (cols. 25–32)	Optimistic estimate for first variable. Decimal point is in column 30; two places of decimals are after decimal point.
Card 5 (cols. 33–40)	Pessimistic estimate for first variable. Decimal point is in column 38; two places of decimals are after decimal point.
Cards 6, 7, 8 . . .	Similar to card 5 but with data for variable numbers 2, 3, 4 . . .

Figure XXVI shows input which could be used for Hertz's well-known case study. The input shows that calculations are to be carried out for three different performance measures: NPV (discount rate = 10%), NPV (discount rate = 20%) and IRR.

```
 1 2 3 4 5 6 7 8 9 10 11 12 13 14 15 16 17 18 19 20 21 22 23 24 25 26 27 28 29 30 31 32 33 34 35 36 37 38 39 40
H E R T Z          M O D E L
             3
             1 0 . 0            2 0 . 0          - 1 0 0 . 0
             9
I N I T  M A R K E T  S I Z E        2 5 0 . 0 0      3 4 0 . 0 0      1 0 0 . 0 0
M A R K E T  G R O W T H                3 . 0 0          6 . 0 0          0 . 0 0
S E L L I N G  P R I C E             5 1 0 . 0 0      5 7 5 . 0 0      3 8 5 . 0 0
M A R K E T  S H A R E                 1 2 . 0 0         1 7 . 0 0          3 . 0 0
I N I T  I N V E S T M E N T      9 5 0 0 . 0 0    7 0 0 0 . 0 0   1 0 5 0 0 . 0 0
L I F E  O F  I N V E S T .            1 0 . 0 0         1 5 . 0 0          5 . 0 0
R E S I D U A L  V A L U E        4 5 0 0 . 0 0    5 0 0 0 . 0 0    3 5 0 0 . 0 0
O P E R A T I N G  C O S T S        4 3 5 . 0 0      3 7 0 . 0 0      5 4 5 . 0 0
F I X E D  C O S T S                3 0 0 . 0 0      2 5 0 . 0 0      3 7 5 . 0 0
```

FIG. XXVI. Input for sensitivity analysis of Hertz's case study

Instead of putting the optimistic estimate for a variable in columns 25–32, and the pessimistic estimate in columns 33–40, the user can do the reverse. The computer will sort out for each variable which of the final two estimates is the optimistic estimate and which is the pessimistic estimate. This facility is designed to give the user the option of reserving columns 25–32 for the larger of the two estimates and columns 33–40 for the smaller of the two estimates.

A.3. The Output

The output consists of a copy of the input data (for subsequent checking) and a sensitivity analysis for each of the performance measures specified by the user. Three different performance measures are specified in Fig. XXVI. The sensitivity analysis output corresponding to the first of these performance measures (i.e. NPV with a discount rate of 10%) is shown in Fig. XXVII.

The variables are arranged in the output in order of decreasing sensitivity. The columns headed "best estimate", "optimistic estimate" and "pessimistic estimate" merely reproduce data provided by the user. The "performance measure at optimistic estimate" column shows the value

HERTZ MODEL

SENSITIVITY ANALYSIS

PERFORMANCE MEASURE = NPV
DISCOUNT RATE = 10.00 PER CENT

VARIABLE NAME	BEST ESTIMATE	OPT. ESTIMATE	PESS. ESTIMATE	PERF. MEAS. AT OPT. EST.	PERF. MEAS. AT PESS. EST.	RANGE OF PERF. MEAS.	RANGE COEFF	PERCENT OF VAR
SELLING PRICE	510.0	575.0	385.0	19303.3	-19934.0	39237.3	1.00	44.14
OPERATING COSTS	435.0	370.0	545.0	19303.3	-16836.4	36139.7	0.92	37.45
MARKET SHARE	12.0	17.0	3.0	12333.5	-5736.3	18069.8	0.46	9.36
INIT MARKET SIZE	250.0	340.0	100.0	11455.8	-341.1	14868.9	0.38	6.34
LIFE OF INVEST	10.0	15.0	5.0	9450.1	1162.8	8287.4	0.21	1.97
MARKET GROWTH	3.0	6.0	0.0	7803.8	4216.9	3587.0	0.09	0.37
INIT INVESTMENT	9500.0	7000.0	10500.0	8380.0	4880.0	3500.0	0.09	0.35
FIXED COSTS	300.0	250.0	375.0	6187.2	5419.2	768.1	0.02	0.02
RESIDUAL VALUE	4500.0	5000.0	3500.0	6072.8	5494.5	578.3	0.01	0.01

VALUE OF PERF. MEAS. WHEN ALL VARIABLES EQUAL THEIR BEST ESTIMATES =   5880.00

VALUE OF PERF. MEAS. WHEN ALL VARIABLES EQUAL THEIR OPTIMISTIC ESTIMATES =   118571.13

VALUE OF PERF. MEAS. WHEN ALL VARIABLES EQUAL THEIR PESSIMISTIC ESTIMATES =   -11567.90

ESTIMATE OF MEAN OF PERF. MEAS. BASED ON PERT ESTIMATES OF THE MEANS OF VARIABLES =   1350.02

ESTIMATE OF S.D. OF PERF. MEAS. BASED ON AN S.D. TO RANGE RATIO OF 0.3 FOR THE VARIABLES =   17717.70

FIG. XXVII. Sensitivity analysis output for Hertz model and discount rate of 10%.

of the performance measure when the variable under consideration is put equal to its optimistic estimate, and all other variables are put equal to their best estimates. Similarly the "performance measure at pessimistic estimate" column shows the value of the performance measure when the variable under consideration is put equal to its pessimistic estimate and all other variables are put equal to their best estimates. The "range of performance measure" column shows the difference between the numbers in the previous two columns. This is termed the sensitivity coefficient in Chapter 5. (It is the range of values of the performance measure which can be produced by varying the value of the variable between its optimistic and pessimistic estimates.) The range coefficient shows the range of the performance measure for the variable under consideration, divided by the range of the performance measure for the most sensitive variable. The final column of the table shows an estimate of the percentage of the variance of the performance measure which is accounted for by different variables. (This is produced on the assumption of linearity as described in Chapter 5.)

The values of the performance measure when all variables are put equal to their best estimates, when all variables are put equal to their optimistic estimates, and when all variables are put equal to their pessimistic estimates are shown under the table on the output (The last two of these are only of limited value as they incorporate rather extreme assumptions.) Also shown under the main table are estimates of the mean and standard deviation of the performance measure. Chapter 5 describes the way in which these estimates are produced. The mean is based on PERT estimates of the means of the individual variables. The standard deviation is based on the assumption:

$$\frac{\text{Standard deviation of variable}}{\text{Difference between optimistic and pessimistic estimates}} = 0.3$$

(The figure 0.3 in this assumption can be changed by making a small modification to the program.)

A.4.   The Subroutine Supplied by the User

In addition to all the standard subroutines (which are listed at the end of the next section) the user must supply his own Fortran subroutine for calculating net cash flows from values of the variables. The title of this subroutine must be MODEL and it must utilise the following variables and arrays:

V(1), V(2) . . .   The values of the variables. V(1) is the value of the first variable specified in the input; V(2) is the value of the second variable specified in the input, etc.

NYEAR   The maximum possible life of the project in years (must be less than 50).

CINIT   The initial (year 0) net cash flow.

C(1), C(2) . . . C(NYEAR) The net cash flows in years 1, 2 . . . NYEAR

Other variables and arrays may be defined by the user as required.

The first two cards of the subroutine must be:

SUBROUTINE MODEL (V)
DIMENSION V(50), C(50)

and after any further DIMENSION statements must come the card:

COMMON/CF/CINIT, C, NYEAR

The subroutine must end as is customary with the statements:

RETURN
END

The array V is passed to the subroutine as a parameter and the essential characteristic of the subroutine must be that it calculates CINIT, C and NYEAR from V.

A simple subroutine MODEL which could be used for the Hertz case study and which was used to produce the output shown in Fig. XXVII is reproduced in Fig. XXVIII.

A.5. The Rest of RISKANAL1

The master segment and standard subroutines which comprise RISKANAL1 are listed at the end of this Appendix. They can be used as they stand or modified to suit the reader's own requirements. The master

```
      SUBROUTINE MODEL(V)
      REAL MKT(50)
      DIMENSION V(20),C(50)
      COMMON /CF/CINIT,C,NYEAR
      NYEAR=V(6)
      CINIT=-V(5)
      MKT(1)=V(1)
      C(1)=V(1)*V(4)*(V(3)-V(8))/100.0-V(9)
      DO 1 IYEAR=2,NYEAR
      MKT(IYEAR)=MKT(IYEAR-1)*(1+V(2)/100.0)
      C(IYEAR)=MKT(IYEAR)*V('4)*(V(3)-V(8))/100.0-V(9)
    1 CONTINUE
      W=V(6)-NYEAR
      IF(W.GT.0.001) GO TO 2
      C(NYEAR)=C(NYEAR)+V(7)
      RETURN
    2 NYEAR=NYEAR+1
      MKT(NYEAR)=MKT(NYEAR-1)*(1+V(2)/100.0)
      C(NYEAR)=V(7)+W*(MKT(NYEAR)*V(4)*(V(3)-V(8))/100.0-V(9))
      RETURN
      END
```

FIG. XXVIII. Subroutine MODEL which is appropriate for Hertz case study.

segment reads and prints out the input data. The definitions of the variables and arrays in the master segment, and the function of that segment, should be apparent from the specification of the input in Section A.2. The master segment calls the subroutines SENSITIVITY, once for each of the discount rates specified by the user.

Brief descriptions of the standard subroutines in RISKANAL1 are as follows:

Sensitivity

This carries out all the calculations for, and prints out, the main sensitivity analysis output. The definitions of the main variables and arrays in SENSITIVITY are as follows:

RATE   The discount rate (passed to the subroutine as a parameter).

PAR (I,1), PAR (I,2),   The three estimates supplied by the user for
PAR (I,3)   variable I (and passed to the subroutine via common block VARDATA).

PESSEST (I)   The pessimistic estimate for variable I (either PAR (I,2) or PAR (I,3)).

OPTEST (I)	The optimistic estimate for variable I (either PAR (I,2) or PAR (I,3)).
PESSPM (I)	The value of the performance measure when variable I is put equal to its pessimistic estimate and all other variables are put equal to their best estimates.
OPTPM (I)	The value of the performance measure when variable I is put equal to its optimistic estimate and all other variables are put equal to their best estimates.
RANGEPM (I)	The difference between OPTPM (I) and PESSPM (I).
MEANEST (I)	The PERT estimate of the mean of variable I.
NVAR	The number of variables.
VARNAME (, I)	The alphabetic name of variable I (16 characters).
ORD (I)	The number of the Ith most sensitive variable.
PMBEST	Value of performance measure based on best estimates.
PMOPT	Value of performance measure based on optimistic estimates.
PMPESS	Value of performance measure based on pessimistic estimates.
PMMN	Estimate of mean of performance measure.
PMSD	Estimate of standard deviation of performance measure.
RANGECOEFF	Range coefficient of variable currently under consideration.
VARPERCENT	Percentage of variance in performance measure accounted for by variable currently under consideration.
V (I)	Value of variable I currently being considered in calculations.
PM1, PM2	Calculated values of the performance measure which are later determined to be PESSPM (I) and OPTPM (I).
SSRANGEPM	Variable in which the sum of the squares of the RANGEPM (I) is accumulated.

PRESVAL

This calculates the net present value of a stream of cash flows. DRATE is the discount rate (passed to the subroutine as a parameter); NPV is the net present value calculated by the subroutine, CINIT, C and NYEAR are as defined in Section A.4.

IRR

This calculates (by successively calling PRESVAL) a percentage internal rate of return for the cash-flow stream described by common block CF using an iterative procedure. RR is the current best estimate of the percentage internal rate of return. The subroutine first calculates values RR1 and RR2 such that the true value of the internal rate of return lies between RR1 and RR2 and RR2 — RR1 = 10. It then successively bisects the interval between RR1 and RR2 so that the true value of the internal rate of return is "homed in" on. If the true internal rate of return is greater than 95% (or if all cash flows are positive) a value of +100 for RR is output. If the true internal rate of return is less than –95% (or if all cash flows are negative) a value of –100 for RR is output. If there is a possibility of multiple IRRs this subroutine should be modified to ensure that the most appropriate IRR is selected.

CALCPM

This directs the program to either PRESVAL or IRR depending on the value of the discount rate currently under consideration. (By convention, a discount rate of –100% indicates that the performance measure IRR should be used.) RATE is the discount rate (input as a parameter to the subroutine); PM is the value of the performance measure calculated by either PRESVAL or IRR.

SORT

This uses a straightforward iterative procedure for arranging in order the numbers VALUES (1), VALUES (2) . . . VALUES (N). The integer array ORD has at the end of the iterations the property that, if J = ORD (I) then VALUES (J) is the Ith highest of the numbers.

A.6. Listing of Standard Subroutines

```
      MASTER RISKANAL1
      REAL VARNAME(2,50),PAR(50,3),TITLE(3),RATE(5)
      COMMON /VARDATA/VARNAME,NVAR,PAR
      READ(1,1) (TITLE(K),K=1,3)
      WRITE(2,5)(TITLE(K),K=1,3)
      WRITE(2,10)
      WRITE(2,6)(TITLE(K),K=1,3)
      READ(1,2) NRATE
      WRITE(2,7)NRATE
      READ(1,3) (RATE(IRATE),IPATE=1,NRATE)
      WRITE(2,8)(RATE(IRATE),IRATE=1,NRATE)
      READ(1,2)NVAR
      WRITE(2,7)NVAR
      DO 100 I=1,NVAR
      READ(1,4)(VARNAME(K,I),K=1,2),(PAR(I,J),J=1,3)
  100 WRITE(2,9)(VARNAME(K,I),K=1,2),(PAR(I,J),J=1,3)
      DO 200 IRATE=1,NRATE
      WRITE(2,5)(TITLE(K),K=1,3).
      R=RATE(IRATE)
  200 CALL SENSITIVITY(R)
    1 FORMAT(3A8)
    2 FORMAT.(I5)
    3 FORMAT(5F10.2)
    4 FORMAT(2A8,3F8.2)
    5 FORMAT(////////////////////////35X,3A8)
    6 FORMAT(1X,3A8)
    7 FORMAT(1X,I5)
    8 FORMAT(1X,5F10.2)
    9 FORMAT(1X,2A8,3F8.2)
   10 FORMAT(15X,18HCOPY OF INPUT DATA/)
      STOP
      END


      SUBROUTINE SENSITIVITY(RATE)
      REAL MEANEST(50),V(50),PAR(50,3)
      REAL PESSPM(50),OPTPM(50),PESSEST(50),OPTEST(50),RANGEPM(50)
      INTEGER ORD(50)
      DIMENSION VARNAME(2,50)
      COMMON /VARDATA/VARNAME,NVAR,PAR
      SSRANGEPM=0
      IF (RATE.LT.-99.0) GO TO 100
      WRITE(2,1) RATE
      GO TO 200
  100 WRITE(2,3)
  200 WRITE(2,2)
      DO 300 I=1,NVAR
  300 V(I)=PAR(I,1)
      CALL MODEL(V)
      CALL CALCPM(RATE,PMBEST)
      DO 400 I=1,NVAR
      V(I)=PAR(I,2)
      CALL MODEL(V)
      CALL CALCPM(RATE,PM1)
      V(I)=PAR(I,3)
      CALL MODEL(V)
      CALL CALCPM(RATE,PM2)
      IF (PM1.GT.PM2) GO TO 500
```

```
         PESSPM(I)=PH1
         OPTPM(I)=PH2
         PESSEST(I)=PAR(I,2)
         OPTEST(I)=PAR(I,3)
         GO TO 600
500      PESSPM(I)=PH2
         OPTPM(I)=PH1
         PESSEST(I)=PAR(I,3)
         OPTEST(I)=PAR(I,2)
600      RANGEPM(I)=OPTPM(I)-PESSPM(I)
         SSRANGEPM=SSRANGEPM+RANGEPM(I)*RANGEPM(I)
         MEANEST(I)=(PAR(I,2)+4.0*PAR(I,1)+PAR(I,3))/6.0
400      V(I)=PAR(I,1)
         CALL SORT(NVAR,RANGEPM,ORD)
         I1=ORD(1)
         DO 700 I=1,NVAR
         J=ORD(I)
         RANGECOEFF=RANGEPM(J)/RANGEPM(I1)
         VARPERCENT=RANGEPM(J)*RANGEPM(J)*100.0/SSRANGEPM
700      WRITE(2,4) (VARNAME(K,J),K=1,2),PAR(J,1),OPTEST(J),PESSEST(J),
        1OPTPM(J),PESSPM(J),RANGEPM(J),RANGECOEFF,VARPERCENT
         CALL MODEL(OPTEST)
         CALL CALCPM(RATE,PMOPT)
         CALL MODEL(PESSEST)
         CALL CALCPM(RATE,PMPESS)
         CALL MODEL(MEANEST)
         CALL CALCPM(RATE,PMMN)
         PMSD=0.3*SQRT(SSRANGEPM)
         WRITE(2,5) P,1BEST,PMOPT,PMPESS,PMMN,PMSD
1        FORMAT(////20X,20HSENSITIVITY ANALYSIS,15X,25HPERFORMANCE MEASURE
        1= NPV/55X,13HDISCOUNT RATE =,F5.2,9H PER CENT)
2        FORMAT(//4X,8HVARIABLE,7X,4HBEST,6X,4HOPT.,6X,5HPESS.,
        13X,11HPERF. MEAS.,4X,11HPERF. MEAS.,4X,
        28HRANGE OF,6X,5HRANGE,3X,7HPERCENT/6X,4HNAME,7X,8HESTIMATE,2X,
        38HESTIMATE,2X,8HESTIMATE,2X,12HAT OPT. EST.,
        42X,13HAT PESS. EST.,2X,11HPERF. MEAS.,4X,5HCOEFF,3X,6HOF VAR/)
3        FORMAT(////20X,20HSENSITIVITY ANALYSIS,15X,25HPERFORMANCE MEASURE
        1= IRR)
4        FORMAT(1X,2A8,F8.1,2X,F8.1,2X,F8.1,2X,F11.1,4X,F11.1,
        13X,F11.1,4X,F6.2,3X,F6.2)
5        FORMAT(///5X,68HVALUE OF PERF. MEAS. WHEN ALL VARIABLES EQUAL THEI
        1R BEST ESTIMATES =,23X,F10.2//5X,74HVALUE OF PERF. MEAS. WHEN ALL
        2VARIABLES EQUAL THEIR OPTIMISTIC ESTIMATES =,17X,F10.2//5X,75HVALU
        3E OF PERF. MEAS. WHEN ALL VARIABLES EQUAL THEIR PESSIMISTIC ESTIMA
        4TES =,16X,F10.2//5X,83HESTIMATE OF MEAN OF PERF. MEAS. BASED ON PE
        5RT ESTIMATES OF THE MEANS OF VARIABLES =, 8X,F10.2//5X,91HESTIMATE
        6 OF S.D. OF PERF. MEAS. BASED ON AN S.D. TO RANGE RATIO OF 0.3 FOR
        7 THE VARIABLES = ,F10.2)
         RETURN
         END


         SUBROUTINE PRESVAL(DRATE,NPV)
         REAL NPV
         DIMENSION C(50)
         COMMON /CF/CINIT,C,NYEAR
         NPV=CINIT
         DISC=1+DRATE/100.0
         DO 10 IYEAR=1,NYEAR
         NPV=NPV+C(IYEAR)/DISC
10       DISC=DISC*(1+DRATE/100.0)
         RETURN
         END
```

```
      SUBROUTINE IRR(RR)
      REAL NPV
      RR=10.0
      CALL PRESVAL(RR,NPV)
      IF (NPV.GT.0) GO TO 20
15    RR2=RR
      RR=RR-10.0
      IF (RR.GT.-95.0) GO TO 25
      RR=-100
      RETURN
25    CALL PRESVAL(RR,NPV)
      IF (NPV.LT.0) GO TO 15
      RR1=RR
      GO TO 30
20    RR1=RR
      RR=RR+10.0
      IF (RR.LT.95.0) GO TO 35
      RR=100
      RETURN
35    CALL PRESVAL(RR,NPV)
      IF (NPV.GT.0) GO TO 20
      RR2=RR
30    DO 45 NCOUNT=1,6
      RR=(RR1+RR2)/2
      CALL PRESVAL(RR,NPV)
      IF (NPV.LT.0) GO TO 40
      RR1=RR
      GO TO 45
40    RR2=RR
45    CONTINUE
      RR=(RR1+RR2)/2
      RETURN
      END


      SUBROUTINE CALCPM(RATE,PH)
      IF(RATE.LT.-99.0) GO TO 1
      CALL PRESVAL(RATE,PH)
      RETURN
1     CALL IRR(PH)
      RETURN
      END


      SUBROUTINE SORT(N,VALUES,ORD)
      INTEGER ORD(50)
      DIMENSION VALUES(50)
      DO 1 I=1,N
1     ORD(I)=I
      DO 2 ICOUNT=1,N-1
      DO 3 I=1,N-1
      J=ORD(I)
      K=ORD(I+1)
      IF (VALUES(J).GT.VALUES(K)) GO TO 4
      ORD(I)=K
      I1=I+1
      ORD(I1)=J
4     CONTINUE
3     CONTINUE
2     CONTINUE
      RETURN
      END
```

Appendix B
A COMPUTER PROGRAM FOR CARRYING OUT RISK SIMULATIONS

B.1. Introduction

The computer program RISKANAL2 described in this Appendix is a series of Fortran subroutines for carrying out risk simulations to produce probability distributions describing the performance of a capital investment project. The user of the program must provide:

(i) Data for each of the variables affecting the performance of the investment; and

(ii) A subroutine for calculating the net cash flows in each year from a given set of values for the variables.

The output from the program consists of a series of graphical displays of the probability distribution of the performance measure.

B.2. The Input

RISKANAL2 can deal with up to fifty variables and carry out the simulations for up to five different performance measures. It can also investigate the effect of up to nine different dependencies between the variables. The performance measure can be either NPV with a specified discount rate or IRR. The desire to use IRR is indicated in the input by the specification of a discount rate of -100%.

The input format as far as the first four cards are concerned is the same as RISKANAL1 (see Section A.2.). The format for card 5 is as follows:

Cols. 1–10   A number between 0 and 67,101,323 to define the random number stream. (Any number in the range can be chosen; if a new random number stream is required at any stage the number should be changed; decimal point is in column 9.)

Cols. 11–15   (Right justified.) The number of simulation runs to be carried out.

Cols. 19–20   (Right justified.) The number of dependencies to be considered.

In card 6 the Nth column contains an integer describing the way in which the Nth variable is to be treated in the simulation and the nature of the data which is to be provided for the Nth variable in the cards which follow. Table 30 shows the meaning of different integers. The integer corresponding to a variable will be referred to as its "type". Thus a variable may be type 1, type 2, type 3 or type 4.

TABLE 30.   THE MEANING OF DIFFERENT INTEGERS

Integer	Meaning
1	Variable is to be described in the simulation by a single estimate which will be provided by the user.
2	Variable is to be described in the simulation by a PERT estimate of its mean which will be based on optimistic, pessimistic and best estimates provided by the user.
3	Variable is to be described in the simulation by a triangular distribution. The mean and standard deviation of the triangular distribution will be equal to PERT estimates of the mean and standard deviation of the variable. These will in turn be based on optimistic, pessimistic and best estimates provided by the user (see Section 5.9. for a description of the methodology.)
4	Variable is to be described in the simulation by a histogram which will be provided by the user.

There then follows data cards for each of the variables taken in order. Type 1, 2 and 3 variables each have 1 data card. Type 4 variables each have two data cards. In the case of type 2 and type 3 variables the format of the data cards is exactly the same as the format of the data cards 5, 6, 7 ... in RISKANAL1 (see Section A.2). In the case of type 1 variables the format of the data card is:

Cols. 1–16   Name of variable (up to sixteen characters).

Cols. 17–24   Best estimate of variable's value. Decimal point in column 22; two places of decimals after decimal point.

In the case of type 4 variables the format of the two data cards is as follows:

1st card

Cols. 1–16   Name of variable (up to sixteen characters).

Col. 20   Number of class intervals on histogram (must be less than or equal to nine.)

Cols. 21–25,   Probabilities of the variable lying in successive class
Cols. 26–30,   intervals starting from extreme left. (Decimal points in
Cols, 31–5 etc.   cols. 23, 28, 33 ... and two places of decimals after decimal points.)

2nd card

Cols. 1–8   The values of the variable at the ends of the class
Cols. 9–16,   intervals starting from the extreme left-hand point of
Cols. 17–24 etc.   the distribution (i.e. the smallest value of the variable) and working towards the right. Decimal points in cols. 6, 14, 22 ... and two places of decimals after each decimal point.

If no dependencies are specified, no further data need be input. Otherwise, one card is required for each dependence with the following format:

Cols. 4–5   (Right justified.) The number of the independent variable

Cols. 9–10   (Right justified.) The number of the dependent variable

Cols. 14–15   (Right justified.) The integer 1 indicates positive dependence is to be considered; the integer −1 indicates negative dependence is to be considered.

Figure XXIX shows input which could be used for Hertz's well-known case study (which is described in Section 3.2). Two of the variables (selling price and operating costs) are type 4, two are type 3, three are type 2 and two are type 1. One thousand simulation runs are to be considered. Two

```
HERTZ   MODEL
        3
        10.00        20.00      -100.00
        9
        1234.0  1000        2
3243221 41
INIT MARKET SIZE    260.00      340.00      100.00
MARKET GROWTH       3.00        6.00        0.00
SELLING PRICE    6  0.10   0.15   0.15   0.25   0.25   0.10
       360.00   400.00   440.00   480.00   520.00   560.00   600.00
MARKET SHARE        12.00       17.00       3.00
INIT INVESTMENT  9500.00    7000.00  10500.00
LIFE OF INVEST.     10.00       15.00       5.00
RESIDUAL VALVE   4500.00
OPERATING COSTS  5  0.20   0.25   0.25   0.20   0.10
       360.00   400.00   440.00   480.00   520.00   560.00
FIXED COSTS         300.00
        1    4    -1
        8    3     1
```

FIG XXIX. Input for RISKANAL2

dependencies (a negative dependence between initial market size and market share and a positive dependence between operating costs and selling price) are to be considered.

As in RISKANAL1, the user can reverse the order of the optimistic and pessimistic estimates when providing data for type 2 or type 3 variables (see Section A.2.) This has been done for some variables in Fig. XXIX.

B.3. The Output

The output consists of a copy of the input data (for subsequent checking) and a series of graphical displays of the probability distributions requested by the user. One probability distribution is produced for each performance measure specified by the user assuming no dependencies. A further set of probability distributions (one for each performance measure) is produced for each dependence specified by the user. Thus the input in Fig. XXIX would lead to a total of nine distributions being produced. Figure XXX shows the first of these distributions (no dependencies; performance measure is NPV with a discount rate of 10%.)

The output is self-explanatory. Suitable class intervals for the

DISTRIBUTION OF NPV, DISCOUNT RATE = 10.00 PER CENT
NO DEPENDENCIES ASSUMED
MEAN= -1162.30   S.D.= 17887.62

RANGE			PROB
LESS THAN	-70000.0		0.0010
-70000.0	TO	-65000.0	0.0000
-65000.0	TO	-60000.0	0.0000
-60000.0	TO	-55000.0	0.0030
-55000.0	TO	-50000.0	0.0010
-50000.0	TO	-45000.0	0.0040
-45000.0	TO	-40000.0	0.0050
-40000.0	TO	-35000.0	0.0090
-35000.0	TO	-30000.0	0.0130
-30000.0	TO	-25000.0	0.0320
-25000.0	TO	-20000.0	0.0390
-20000.0	TO	-15000.0	0.0710
-15000.0	TO	-10000.0	0.1110
-10000.0	TO	-5000.0	0.1400
-5000.0	TO	0.0	0.1080
0.0	TO	5000.0	0.0940
5000.0	TO	10000.0	0.0600
10000.0	TO	15000.0	0.0450
15000.0	TO	20000.0	0.0310
20000.0	TO	25000.0	0.0270
25000.0	TO	30000.0	0.0220
30000.0	TO	35000.0	0.0080
35000.0	TO	40000.0	0.0160
40000.0	TO	45000.0	0.0030
45000.0	TO	50000.0	0.0030
50000.0	TO	55000.0	0.0030
55000.0	TO	60000.0	0.0010
60000.0	TO	65000.0	0.0010
65000.0	TO	70000.0	0.0000
70000.0	TO	75000.0	0.0000
GREATER THAN	80000.0		0.0020

FIG. XXX   Output from RISKANAL2

distributions are determined on the basis of the first 100 simulations (or on the basis of the total number of simulations if this less than 100). When a dependence between two variables is considered, total positive or negative dependence, as defined in Section 4.3 is assumed.

B.4.   The Subroutine Supplied By The User

In addition to the standard subroutines, the user must supply his own Fortran subroutine for calculating net cash flows from values of the variables. This is precisely the same as the corresponding subroutine in RISKANAL1 (see Section A.4) and the subroutine shown in Fig. XXVIII is the one used to produce Figure XXX.

B.5.   The Rest of RISKANAL2

RISKANAL2 utilises the subroutines PRESVAL, IRR and CALCPM which were described in Section A.5 and listed at the end of Appendix A. The master segment and the remainder of the subroutines comprising RISKANAL2 are listed at the end of this Appendix. They can be used as they stand or modified to suit the user's own requirements.

The definitions of most of the variables and arrays in the master segment, and the general operation of that segment should be apparent from the specification of the input in Section B.2. If variable I is type 2, MEAN (I) is calculated as the PERT estimate of the value of variable I. If variable I is type 3 the subroutine TRIANGPAR is used to calculate suitable parameters for the triangular distribution from optimistic, pessimistic and best estimates of the value of variable I. (MT(I) is the mode of the triangular distribution; AT(I) is its lower bound; BT(I) is its upper bound). If variable I is type 4 the parameters of a histogram are recorded in arrays NINT, PROB and VALUE. The master segment calls subroutine CONTROL.

Brief descriptions of the standard subroutines in RISKANAL2 are as follows:

Control

After initialising a number of arrays, this subroutine carries out a number of preliminary simulation runs by repeatedly calling subroutine

SIM. (The number of initial simulation runs is 100 or the number of simulation runs specified by the user in the input if this is less than 100.) It then calculates means and standard deviations for the performance measures from these preliminary simulations and calls GRAPHPAR in order to determine suitable class intervals for the histograms which are to be output. (A different set of class intervals is determined for each of the different performance measures considered.) After assigning the values of the performance measures already simulated to the class intervals (by calling a subroutine COLLECT), it then carries out the remainder of the simulation runs required by the user (if any) assigning the values of the performance measures to class intervals as it goes along. Finally, it calls subroutines HEADING and GRAPHPLOT to produce the output.

The definitions of the main variables used in CONTROL are:

IDEP	Counts the different simulations. IDEP = 1 denotes the simulation in which no dependencies are considered. Otherwise IDEP denotes the simulation in which dependence number (IDEP − 1) is considered.
IRATE	Counts the different performance measures considered.
IRUN	Counts the simulation runs.
L	Counts class intervals on output histograms.
SUMPM (IDEP, IRATE)	Sums simulated values of the performance measure IRATE for simulation number IDEP.
SUMSQPM (IDEP, IRATE)	Sums squares of simulated values of the performance measure IRATE for simulation number IDEP.
NOBS (L, IDEP, IRATE)	Number of simulated values of performance measure number IRATE in Lth class interval for simulation number IDEP.
INITRUNS	Number of simulation runs initially carried out.
PM (IDEP, IRATE)	Simulated values of performance measure.

PMVAL (IRUN, IDEP, (IRATE)	Simulated values of performance measure — remembered for initial simulation runs.
MU, SIGMA	Mean and standard deviation of performance measure calculated on the basis of initial simulation runs.
START (IRATE)	Starting value for output histograms corresponding to performance measure number IRATE.
WIDTH (IRATE)	Width of class intervals for output histograms corresponding to performance measure number IRATE.
NWIDTH (IRATE)	Number of class intervals for output histograms corresponding to performance measure number IRATE.

SIM

The subroutine SIM carries out a single run of each of the simulations requested by the user each time it is called. It starts by using subroutine RANDOM to sample independent random numbers RAND(I) between 0 and 1 for each variable I. It then uses subroutine SAMPLE to find a value V(I) equal to the RAND(I) fractile of the distribution of I. (V(I) is therefore a random sample from the distribution of variable I.) The subroutine then calls CALCPM in order to calculate values for the performance measures corresponding to the V(I). Each dependence between a dependent variable I2 and an independent variable I1 is then considered in turn. If variable I2 is positively dependent on variable I1 a further simulation is carried out with V (I2) equal to the RAND(I1) fractile of the distribution of variable 12. If variable I2 is negatively dependent on variable I1 a further simulation is carried out with V(I2) equal to the 1 – RAND(I1) fractile of the distribution of variable I2. The definitions of other variables used are as follows:

PM (IDEP, IRATE)	Value calculated for performance measure in simulation number IDEP with performance measure number IRATE (see subroutine CONTROL for definitions of IDEP and IRATE.)

RP   Parameter used to generate random numbers. Its
                  initial value is supplied in the input.
RATE (IRATE)   Discount rate in performance measure number
                  IRATE.

GRAPHPAR

This subroutine determines suitable class intervals for a distribution with
mean MU and standard deviation SIGMA. START, WIDTH and
NWIDTH are the parameters calculated by GRAPHPAR. START is the
beginning of the first-class interval, WIDTH is the width of the class
intervals and NWIDTH is the number of class intervals. WIDTH is
approximately equal to $0.2 \times$ SIGMA and is actually chosen as 10^n,
2×10^n or 5×10^n for same positive or negative integer n. START is a
multiple of WIDTH approximately equal to MU – 4 * SIGMA. NWIDTH
is chosen so that the class intervals cover the range between MU – 4 *
SIGMA and MU + 4 * SIGMA.

COLLECT

START, WIDTH, NWIDTH and NOBS are as defined in CONTROL.
This subroutine tests which class interval of a given distribution a given
number X lies in and adds one to the cumulative total of observations in that
class interval.

HEADING

This subroutine prints out a heading for the distribution corresponding
to simulation number IDEP and performance measure number IRATE.
(see subroutine CONTROL for definitions of IDEP and IRATE.

GRAPHPLOT

This subroutine prints out a display of the distribution corresponding to
simulation number IDEP and performance measure number IRATE (see
subroutine CONTROL for definitions of IDEP and IRATE). A scaling
factor, SCALEFACTOR, is calculated to ensure that there are a maximum

of about 500 crosses in total on the display. COPY (K,A,I,B,J) is a special ICL routine (which the user may have to supply himself) for copying K characters from array A to array B starting at the *I*th character in A and the *J*th character in B.

RANDOM

This subroutine calculates a random number, RAND, between 0 and 1. It also updates a parameter, P, which is used in the calculations. This random number generator is described in Downham and Roberts (1967).

TRIANGULAR

In this subroutine M, A and B are the best estimate, pessimistic estimate and optimistic estimate for a variable. MEAN and SD are PERT estimates for the mean and standard deviation of the variable. MT, AT and BT are the mode, lower bound and upper bound of a triangular distribution which has mean, MEAN, and standard deviation, SD. The calculations are described in Section 5.9. The equality

$$\frac{MT - AT}{BT - MT} = \frac{M - A}{B - A}$$

is built into the calculations

TRIANGSAMPLE

This subroutine calculates the value V which is equal to the Rth fractile of a triangular distribution with mode M, lower bound A and upper bound B.

HISTOSAMPLE

This subroutine calculates the value V which is equal to the RAND fractile of the histogram defined by the parameters NINT, PB and VL. NINT is the number of class intervals. PB(J) is the probability of the variable lying in the Jth class interval. VL(J) and VL(J+1) are the end points of the Jth class interval.

SAMPLE

This subroutine finds the value V which corresponds to the RAND fractile of the distribution of variable I. It first tests whether the variable is type 1, type 2, type 3 or type 4 (see Section B.2). If the variable is type 1 or type 2 it immediately puts it equal to MEAN(I). If the variable is type 3 it calls TRIANGSAMPLE. If the variable is type 4 it calls HISTOSAMPLE.

Reference

DOWNHAM, D. Y. and ROBERTS, F. D. K. (1967). Multiplicative congruential pseudo-random number generators, *The Computer Journal*, vol. 16, no. 1, pp.74–7.

```
      MASTER RISKANAL2
      REAL TITLE(3),RATE(5),VARNAME(2,50),MEAN(50),VALUE(10,50)
      REAL M(50),A(50),B(50),HT(50),AT(50),BT(50),PROB(9,50)
      INTEGER TYPE(50),NINT(50),DEPTYPE(10),IND(10),DEP(10)
      COMMON /DATA/NRUN,NRATE,NDEP,NVAR
      COMMON /NAMES/VARNAME
      COMMON /DEPDATA/IND,DEP,DEPTYPE
      COMMON /DISTDATA/MEAN,PROB,VALUE,NINT,TYPE,HT,AT,BT
      COMMON /RATEDATA/RATE
      READ(1,1) (TITLE(K),K=1,3)
      WRITE(2,5)(TITLE(K),K=1,3)
      WRITE(2,10)
      WRITE(2,6)(TITLE(K),K=1,3)
      READ(1,2) NRATE
      WRITE(2,7)NRATE
      READ(1,3) (RATE(IRATE),IRATE=1,NRATE)
      WRITE(2,8)(RATE(IRATE),IRATE=1,NRATE)
      READ(1,2) NVAR
      WRITE(2,7)NVAR
      READ(1,4) RP,NRUN,NDEP
      WRITE(2,9)RP,NRUN,NDEP
      READ(1,11)(TYPE(I),I=1,NVAR)
      WRITE(2,12)(TYPE(I),I=1,NVAR)
      DO 100 I=1,NVAR
      NT=TYPE(I)
      GO TO (20,30,40,50)NT
   20 READ(1,13) (VARNAME(K,I),K=1,2),MEAN(I)
      WRITE(2,14)(VARNAME(K,I),K=1,2),MEAN(I)
      GO TO 100
   30 READ(1,13) (VARNAME(K,I),K=1,2),M(I),A(I),B(I)
      WRITE(2,14)(VARNAME(K,I),K=1,2),M(I),A(I),B(I)
      MEAN(I)=(A(I)+4.0*M(I)+B(I))/6.0
      GO TO 100
   40 READ(1,13) (VARNAME(K,I),K=1,2),M(I),A(I),B(I)
      WRITE(2,14)(VARNAME(K,I),K=1,2),M(I),A(I),B(I)
      CALL TRIANGPAR(M(I),A(I),B(I),HT(I),AT(I),BT(I))
      GO TO 100
   50 READ(1,15) (VARNAME(K,I),K=1,2),NINT(I),(PROB(INT,I),INT=1,NINT(I)
     1)
      READ(1,16) (VALUE(INT,I),INT=1,NINT(I)+1)
      WRITE(2,17)(VARNAME(K,I),K=1,2),NINT(I),(PROB(INT,I),INT=1,NINT(I)
     1)
      WRITE(2,18)(VALUE(INT,I),INT=1,NINT(I)+1)
  100 CONTINUE
      IF(NDEP.EQ.0) GO TO 200
      DO 300 IDEP=2,NDEP+1
      READ(1,2) IND(IDEP),DEP(IDEP),DEPTYPE(IDEP)
  300 WRITE(2,7)IND(IDEP),DEP(IDEP),DEPTYPE(IDEP)
  200 CALL CONTROL(RP)
    1 FORMAT(3A8)
    2 FORMAT(10I5)
    3 FORMAT(8F10.2)
    4 FORMAT(F10.1,2I5)
    5 FORMAT(////////////////////////35X,3A8)
    6 FORMAT(1X,3A8)
    7 FORMAT(1X,10I5)
    8 FORMAT(1X,8F10.2)
    9 FORMAT(1X,F10.1,2I5)
   10 FORMAT(15X,18HCOPY OF INPUT DATA/)
   11 FORMAT(50I1)
   12 FORMAT(1X,50I1)
   13 FORMAT(2A8,3F8.2)
   14 FORMAT(1X,2A8,3F8.2)
   15 FORMAT(2A8,I4,9F5.2)
   16 FORMAT(10F8.2)
   17 FORMAT(1X,2A8,I4,9F5.2)
   18 FORMAT(1X,10F8.2)
      STOP
      END
```

```
      SUBROUTINE CONTROL(RP)
      REAL SUMPM(11,5),SUMSQPM(11,5),PMVAL(100,11,5),PM(11,5),MU
      REAL START(5),WIDTH(5)
      INTEGER NWIDTH(5),NOBS(80,11,5)
      COMMON /DATA/NRUN,NRATE,NDEP,NVAR
      COMMON /STATS/SUMPM,SUMSQPM
      COMMON /DISTPMDATA/START,WIDTH,NWIDTH,NOBS
      DO 10 IRATE=1,NRATE
      DO 10 IDEP=1,NDEP+1
      SUMPM(IDEP,IRATE)=0
      SUMSQPM(IDEP,IRATE)=0
      DO 10 L=1,80
10    NOBS(L,IDEP,IRATE)=0
      INITRUNS=MINO(100,NRUN)
      DO 20 IRUN=1,INITRUNS
      CALL SIM(RP,PM)
      DO 20 IRATE=1,NRATE
      DO 20 IDEP=1,NDEP+1
      PMVAL(IRUN,IDEP,IRATE)=PM(IDEP,IRATE)
      SUMPM(IDEP,IRATE)=SUMPM(IDEP,IRATE)+PM(IDEP,IRATE)
      SUMSQPM(IDEP,IRATE)=SUMSQPM(IDEP,IRATE)+
20    1PM(IDEP,IRATE)*PM(IDEP,IRATE)
      DO 30 IRATE=1,NRATE
      S=SUMPM(1,IRATE)
      SS=SUMSQPM(1,IRATE)
      MU=S/INITRUNS
      SIGMA=SQRT(SS/(INITRUNS-1)-S*S/(INITRUNS*(INITRUNS-1)))
      CALL GRAPHPAR(MU,SIGMA,START(IRATE),WIDTH(IRATE),NWIDTH(IRATE))
      DO 30 IDEP=1,NDEP+1
      DO 30 IRUN=1,INITRUNS
30    CALL COLLECT(IDEP,IRATE,PMVAL(IRUN,IDEP,IRATE))
      IF (NRUN.LE. 100) GO TO 60
      DO 40 IRUN=1,NRUN-INITRUNS
      CALL SIM(RP,PM)
      DO 40 IRATE=1,NRATE
      DO 40 IDEP=1,NDEP+1
      SUMPM(IDEP,IRATE)=SUMPM(IDEP,IRATE)+PM(IDEP,IRATE)
      SUMSQPM(IDEP,IRATE)=SUMSQPM(IDEP,IRATE)+
      1PM(IDEP,IRATE)*PM(IDEP,IRATE)
40    CALL COLLECT(IDEP,IRATE,PM(IDEP,IRATE))
60    DO 50 IRATE=1,NRATE
      DO 50 IDEP=1,NDEP+1
      CALL HEADING(IDEP,IRATE)
50    CALL GRAPHPLOT(IDEP,IRATE)
      RETURN
      END
```

```
      SUBROUTINE SIM(RP,PH)
      REAL RAND(50),V(50),RATE(5),PH(11,5)
      INTEGER IND(10),DEP(10),DEPTYPE(10)
      COMMON /DEPDATA/IND,DEP,DEPTYPE
      COMMON /RATEDATA/RATE
      COMMON /DATA/NRUN,NRATE,NDEP,NVAR
      DO 10 I=1,NVAR
      CALL RANDOM(RP,RAND(I))
10    CALL SAMPLE(I,RAND(I),V(I))
      CALL MODEL(V)
      DO 20 IRATE=1,NRATE
20    CALL CALCPH(RATE(IRATE),PH(1,IRATE))
      IF(NDEP.GT.0) GO TO 30
      RETURN
30    DO 40 IDEP=2,NDEP+1
      I1=IND(IDEP)
      I2=DEP(IDEP)
      VDUM=V(I2)
      IF(DEPTYPE(IDEP).EQ.-1) GO TO 50
      CALL SAMPLE(I2,RAND(I1),V(I2))
      GO TO 60
50    RINV=1-RAND(I1)
      CALL SAMPLE(I2,RINV,V(I2))
60    CALL MODEL(V)
      DO 70 IRATE=1,NRATE
70    CALL CALCPH(RATE(IRATE),PH(IDEP,IRATE))
      V(I2)=VDUM
40    CONTINUE
      RETURN
      END
```

```
      SUBROUTINE GRAPHPAR(MU,SIGMA,START,WIDTH,NWIDTH)
      REAL MU
      IF (SIGMA.GT.0) GO TO 5
      START=MU
      WIDTH=1
      NWIDTH=1
      RETURN
5     X=SIGMA/5.0
      IF(X.GT.1.0) GO TO 1
      FACTOR=0.1
      X=X*10.0
20    IF (X.GT.1.0) GO TO 10
      FACTOR=FACTOR*0.1
      X=X*10.0
      GO TO 20
1     FACTOR=1.0
30    IF (X.LT.10.0) GO TO 10
      X=0.1*X
      FACTOR=FACTOR*10.0
      GO TO 30
10    IF (X.GT.1.5) GO TO 40
      Z=1.0
      GO TO 100
40    IF (X.GT.3.5) GO TO 50
      Z=2.0
      GO TO 100
50    IF (X.GT.7.5) GO TO 60
      Z=5.0
      GO TO 100
60    Z=10.0
100   WIDTH=Z*FACTOR
      Y=MU-4.0*SIGMA
      N=Y/WIDTH
      START=N*WIDTH
      Y=MU+4.0*SIGMA
      N1=Y/WIDTH+1.0
      NWIDTH=N1-N+1
      RETURN
      END




      SUBROUTINE COLLECT(IDEP,IRATE,X)
      REAL START(5),WIDTH(5)
      INTEGER NWIDTH(5),NOBS(80,11,5)
      COMMON /DISTPMDATA/START,WIDTH,NWIDTH,NOBS
      S=START(IRATE)
      W=WIDTH(IRATE)
      NW=NWIDTH(IRATE)
      L=1
7     IF (X.LT.S+(L-1)*W) GO TO 4
      IF (L.EQ.NW) GO TO 4
      L=L+1
      GO TO 7
4     NOBS(L,IDEP,IRATE)=NOBS(L,IDEP,IRATE)+1
      RETURN
      END
```

```
      SUBROUTINE HEADING(IDEP,IRATE)
      REAL RATE(5),VARNAME(2,50)
      INTEGER DEPTYPE(10),IND(10),DEP(10)
      COMMON /NAMES/VARNAME
      COMMON /DEPDATA/IND,DEP,DEPTYPE
      COMMON /RATEDATA/RATE
      IF(RATE(IRATE).LT.-99.0) GO TO 10
      WRITE(2,1) RATE(IRATE)
      GO TO 20
10    WRITE(2,2)
20    IF(IDEP.EQ.1) GO TO 30
      I1=IND(IDEP)
      I2=DEP(IDEP)
      IF(DEPTYPE(IDEP).EQ.-1) GO TO 40
      WRITE(2,3) (VARNAME(K,I2),K=1,2),(VARNAME(K,I1),K=1,2)
      RETURN
40    WRITE(2,4) (VARNAME(K,I2),K=1,2),(VARNAME(K,I1),K=1,2)
      RETURN
30    WRITE(2,5)
1     FORMAT(//////////////40X,37HDISTRIBUTION OF NPV. DISCOUNT RATE = ,F
     15.2,9H PER CENT)
2     FORMAT(//////////////40X,19HDISTRIBUTION OF IRR)
3     FORMAT(5X,2A8,47H ASSUMED TO BE TOTALLY POSITIVELY DEPENDENT ON ,
     12A8)
4     FORMAT(5X,2A8,47H ASSUMED TO BE TOTALLY NEGATIVELY DEPENDENT ON ,
     12A8)
5     FORMAT(40X,23HNO DEPENDENCIES ASSUMED)
      RETURN
      END
```

```
SUBROUTINE GRAPHPLOT(IDEP,IRATE)
REAL SUMPM(11,5),SUMSQPM(11,5),START(5),WIDTH(5),MEAN
INTEGER NWIDTH(5),NOBS(80,11,5),TOTRUN
DIMENSION A(15),B(15),C(15)
COMMON /DISTPMDATA/START,WIDTH,NWIDTH,NOBS
COMMON /STATS/SUMPM,SUMSQPM
COMMON /DATA/NRUN,NRATE,NDEP,NVAR
DATA A(1)/120H
1
2 /
DATA B(1)/120HXXXXXXXXXXXXXXXXXXXXXXXXXXXXXXXXXXXXXXXXXXXXXXXXXXX
1XXXXXXXXXXXXXXXXXXXXXXXXXXXXXXXXXXXXXXXXXXXXXXXXXXXXXXXXXXXXXXXXXXX
2XX/
S=SUMPM(IDEP,IRATE)
SS=SUMSQPM(IDEP,IRATE)
MEAN=S/NRUN
SD=SQRT(SS/(NRUN-1)-S*S/(NRUN*(NRUN-1)))
WRITE(2,1) MEAN,SD
WRITE(2,2)
IF(NRUN.LT.500) GO TO 50
SCALEFACTOR=500.0/NRUN
GO TO 60
50    SCALEFACTOR=1.0
60    CONTINUE
N=NOBS(1,IDEP,IRATE)*SCALEFACTOR+0.5
CALL COPY(120,C(1),1,A(1),1)
IF (N.EQ.0) GO TO 20
CALL COPY(N,C(1),1,B(1),1)
20    CONTINUE
RN=NOBS(1,IDEP,IRATE)
AF=RN/NRUN
WRITE(2,3) START(IRATE),AF,(C(I),I=1,10)
DO 70 L=2,NWIDTH(IRATE)-1
X2=START(IRATE)+(L-1)*WIDTH(IRATE)
X1=X2-WIDTH(IRATE)
N=NOBS(L,IDEP,IRATE)*SCALEFACTOR+0.5
CALL COPY(120,C(1),1,A(1),1)
IF (N.EQ.0) GO TO 30
CALL COPY(N,C(1),1,B(1),1)
30    CONTINUE
RN=NOBS(L,IDEP,IRATE)
AF=RN/NRUN
WRITE(2,4) X1,X2,AF,(C(I),I=1,10)
70    CONTINUE
X2=START(IRATE)+(NWIDTH(IRATE)-1)*WIDTH(IRATE)
NW=NWIDTH(IRATE)
N=NOBS(NW,IDEP,IRATE)*SCALEFACTOR+0.5
CALL COPY(120,C(1),1,A(1),1)
IF (N.EQ.0) GO TO 40
CALL COPY(N,C(1),1,B(1),1)
40    CONTINUE
RN=NOBS(NW,IDEP,IRATE)
AF=RN/NRUN
WRITE(2,5) X2,AF,(C(I),I=1,10)
1     FORMAT(40X,5HMEAN=,F10.2,5X,5HS.D.=,F10.2/)
2     FORMAT(10X,5HRANGE,12X,4HPROB/)
3     FORMAT(5X,9HLESS THAN,F10.1,F8.4,3X,1HI,10A8)
4     FORMAT (F10.1,2X,2HTO,F10.1,F8.4,5X,1HI,10A8)
5     FORMAT(2X,12HGREATER THAN,F10.1,F8.4,3X,1HI,10A8)
RETURN
END
```

```
SUBROUTINE RANDOM(P,RAND)
DOUBLE PRECISION X,Q
X=P
X=3.192D+3*X
K=X/6.7101323D+7
Q=K
Q=Q*6.7101323D+7
X=X-Q
RAND=X/67101323.
P=X
RETURN
END


SUBROUTINE TRIANGPAR(M,A,B,MT,AT,BT)
REAL MEAN,M,MT
MEAN=(A+4*M+B)/6.0
SD=ABS(B-A)*0.3
X=(B-M)/(M-A)
Y=SD*SQRT(18.0/(1+X*X*X))
MT=M-Y*(X-1)/3.0
AT=MT-Y
BT=MT+X*Y
RETURN
END


SUBROUTINE TRIANGSAMPLE(R,M,A,B,V)
REAL M
        IF (R.LT.((M-A)/(B-A))) GO TO 100
        V=B-SQRT((B-M)*(B-A)*(1-R))
        GO TO 150
100     V=A+SQRT(R*(M-A)*(B-A))
150     CONTINUE
RETURN
END


SUBROUTINE HISTOSAMPLE(RAND,NINT,PB,VL,V)
REAL PB(9),VL(10)
CUMPB=0
J=1
10      CUMPB=CUMPB+PB(J)
        IF(CUMPB.GT.RAND) GO TO 20
        J=J+1
        GO TO 10
20      V=(VL(J)*(CUMPB-RAND)+VL(J+1)*(RAND-CUMPB+PB(J)))/PB(J)
RETURN
END


SUBROUTINE SAMPLE(I,RAND,V)
REAL MT(50),AT(50),BT(50),PB(11),VL(11)
REAL MEAN(50),PROB(9,50),VALUE(10,50),SD(50)
INTEGER NINT(50),TYPE(50)
COMMON /DISTDATA/MEAN,PROB,VALUE,NINT,TYPE,MT,AT,BT
K=TYPE(I)
        GO TO (10,10,30,40) K
10      V=MEAN(I)
        RETURN
30      CALL TRIANGSAMPLE(RAND,MT(I),AT(I),BT(I),V)
        RETURN
40      DO 100 L=1,NINT(I)+1
        PB(L)=PROB(L,I)
100     VL(L)=VALUE(L,I)
        CALL HISTOSAMPLE(RAND,NINT(I),PB,VL,V)
RETURN
END
```

Appendix C
A SAMPLING SCHEME FOR DEALING WITH DEPENDENT VARIABLES

C.1. Introduction

This Appendix provides the theory behind the sampling scheme which is briefly outlined in Section 4.7 for dealing with dependence. A fuller discussion of the theory with an example can be found in Hull (1977).

C.2. Underlying Theory

Define

V_2	dependent variable
V_1	independent variable
$g(V_2)$	unconditional distribution of V_2
$f(V_1)$	distribution of V_1
$h(V_2/V_1)$	distribution of V_2 conditional on V_1

For consistency we must have

$$g(V_2) = \int_{-\infty}^{+\infty} h(V_2/V_1) f(V_1)\, dV_1 \qquad (C.1)$$

This appendix will show how to obtain distributions h which satisfy Equation (C.1) and are consistent with a simple estimate of dependence of the form: if $V_1 = \ldots$, the median estimate for $V_2 = \ldots$. The theory is based transforming the multivariate normal distribution.

First we note that if f and g are both $N(0,1)$

$$h(V_2/V_1) \sim N(\rho V_1, 1-\rho^2)$$

satisfies Equation (C.1) where ρ is the coefficient of correlation between V_1 and V_2. This result is a straightforward application of the theory of multivariate normal distributions.

In general, V_1 and V_2 will not be normal. However, they can always be transformed to the normal distribution $N(0,1)$ on a "fractile to fractile" basis. Define functions z and w which are such that $z(V_1)$ and $w(V_2)$ are both $N(0,1)$. The distributions f and g are then:

$$f(V_1) = \frac{dz}{dV_1} \, \phi \, [z(V_1)]$$

$$g(V_2) = \frac{dw}{dV_2} \, \phi \, [w(V_2)]$$

where ϕ is $N(0,1)$. If h is given by:

$$h \, (V_2/V_1) = \frac{dw}{dV_2} \, \phi \, [w(V_2)]$$

where ϕ is $N(\rho z(V_1), \, 1-\rho^2)$ then it follows from the multivariate normal distribution result given above that Equation (C.1) is satisfied.

The distribution $h(V_2/V_1)$ is therefore obtained by applying the transformation w^{-1} to the normal distribution $N(\rho z(V_1), 1-\rho^2)$. ρ it should be noted is the coefficient of correlation between $z(V_1)$ and $w(V_2)$ not that between V_1 and V_2.

C.3.   Sampling Scheme

An estimate for ρ can be obtained if a single assessment of the form:

"assuming $V_1 = Q$, my median estimate for V_2 is P"

is made. To show why this is so we note that $w(P)$ is the 0.50 fractile of $N(\rho z(Q), 1-\rho^2)$, i.e.

$$w(P) = \rho z(Q)$$

i.e. $$\rho \quad = \frac{w(P)}{z(Q)}$$

Generally, an analyst will wish to obtain two or three assessments of the form: if $V_1 = Q$, the median $V_2 = P$ and average the estimates of ρ which are obtained. Any value except the median of V_1 can in theory be used for Q. Once ρ has been obtained the following sampling scheme is appropriate:

(i) Sample a value q_1 from $N(0,1)$.
(ii) Sample a value q_2 from $N(0,1)$ such that the coefficient of correlation between q_1 and q_2 is ρ.
(iii) Calculate the fractile (say j_1) of $N(0,1)$ to which q_1 corresponds and the fractile (say j_2) of $N(0,1)$ to which q_2 corresponds.
(iv) Put the V_1 sample equal to the j_1th fractile of its distribution and the V_2 sample equal to the j_2th fractile of its distribution.

C.4.   Application to Time Dependencies

The model which has been presented can be used to solve the growth-rate problem (see Section 4.8). Suppose:

x_i is the value of the variable in time period i,

$f_i(x_i)$ is the unconditional probability distribution of x_i,

$h_i(x_i/x_{i-1})$ is the conditional distribution of x_i given x_{i-1}.

Then, once f_{i-1} and f_i have been determined, distributions h_i can be estimated in a similar way to that described in Sections C.2 and C.3 using assessments of the form:

"assuming the value of the variable in year i-1 is Q, the median estimate for year i is P".

To reduce the overall number of assessments which have to be made to manageable proportions the analyst will no doubt find it desirable to assume:

(a) that all the f_i have the same basic shape with only the mean and variance changing as i changes; and
(b) that the parameter necessary to determine h_i (defined as ρ in Section C.2) remains the same for all values of i.

Reference

HULL, J. C. (1977). Dealing with dependence in risk simulations, *Operational Research Quarterly*, vol. 28, lii, pp. 201–13.